100
soups
from 1 easy recipe

100 soups

from 1 easy recipe

LOVE FOOD™

This edition published in 2011

LOVE FOOD is an imprint of Parragon Books Ltd

Parragon
Queen Street House
4 Queen Street
Bath BA1 1HE, UK

ISBN: 978-1-4454-6260-8

Printed in China

Cover design by Talking Design
Written by Linda Doeser
Internal design by Simon Levy
Photography by Mike Cooper
Home economy by Lincoln Jefferson

Notes for the Reader
This book uses standard kitchen measuring spoons and cups. All spoon and cup measurements are level unless otherwise indicated. Unless otherwise stated, milk is assumed to be whole, eggs are large, individual vegetables are medium, and pepper is freshly ground black pepper.

The times given are only an approximate guide. Preparation times differ according to the techniques used by different people and the cooking times may also vary from those given. Optional ingredients, variations, or serving suggestions have not been included in the calculations.

Recipes using raw or very lightly cooked eggs should be avoided by infants, the elderly, pregnant women, convalescents, and anyone with a chronic illness. Pregnant and breast-feeding women are advised to avoid eating peanuts and peanut products. People with nut allergies should be aware that some of the prepared ingredients used in the recipes in this book may contain nuts. Always check the packaging before use.

Contents

Introduction

It must have been a great, if unsung, moment in the history of civilization when one of our enterprising prehistoric ancestors first put some roots and aromatics into a pot of water and heated it over a fire. Although today's cooking methods are somewhat less primitive and ingredients are more sophisticated and varied, soup remains one of the easiest dishes to prepare, while still being tasty, nourishing, versatile, easy to digest, and the ultimate comfort food.

Soups may be served hot or chilled, they can be a first course or a meal-in-a bowl, they may be hearty and rustic, elegant and subtle, thick and creamy, or delicate and clear, and can incorporate almost every imaginable ingredient from meat and poultry to vegetables and fruit and from cheese and eggs to fish and shellfish. Virtually every cuisine in the world features at least one—and usually many—soup recipes based on local ingredients and preferences.

The hundred recipes in this book celebrate the immense versatility of soup. Whatever your taste and whatever the occasion, you are sure to find a recipe to suit you. If you're looking for a first course for a dinner party, try Stylish Soups with its collection of clear broths and special flavors or, if it's summer time, Cool Soups with both familiar and unusual chilled delights.

Hearty Soups offers a profusion of great ideas for economical yet satisfying family meals, while Tasty Soups are perfect winter warmers and restoratives for anyone feeling under the weather. For an international flavor, turn to World Classics, which features recipes as varied as a simple yet delicious Greek egg and lemon soup, an unusual sweet and sour onion soup from Iran, Thailand's spicy signature dish Tom Yam Goong, and a bacon and split pea soup from England. All of the recipes are easy to follow, many of them are surprisingly quick to prepare, all of them taste fabulous, and, best of all, they are all based on one basic vegetable stock (see page 10).

Making and adapting stock

Obviously, any soup can be made using water as the basic liquid and a few fairly unusual recipes always are. However, as a general rule, the flavor is enriched and intensified with a good-quality stock, which also adds to the nutritional value and helps give "eye appeal." Stock can be made from many different ingredients, and restaurant kitchens will have at least a basic collection of chicken, beef, and possibly other meat, fish, shellfish, and vegetable stocks at hand. This would be demanding for even the most enthusiastic home cook, and as most of us are preparing only family meals, an entire freezer would have to be allocated to their storage.

Vegetable stock has been chosen as the basis of the soups in this book for a variety of reasons. It is relatively unusual for any soup, whether featuring chicken, meat, fish, mushrooms, sausages, or whatever, not to include some vegetables, so it will always go well with other ingredients. Of course, some of the best-loved soups are, in any case, vegetable broths. While it is flavorful, it is not so strong that it will overpower other delicate ingredients. It is acceptable to both meat eaters and vegetarians. Finally, it is easier, more economical, and quicker to make a tasty vegetable stock than any other type.

The basic recipe is for what is known as a light stock, meaning its color not its flavor, and it is suitable for all the soups in the book (and many others). The ingredients are widely available and inexpensive, but you can substitute other vegetables if you particularly dislike one ingredient, you have others at hand or you want to enhance the flavor of a special soup for a particular occasion. All members of the onion family can be used, as well as those suggested. Both fresh and dried mushrooms will add an earthy flavor that some people relish, while others appreciate the sweetness imparted by corn. However, some vegetables should be used with caution. Any members of the cabbage family, including Brussels sprouts and kohlrabi, are likely to overpower other flavors. Fennel has a distinctive aniseed flavor that won't go with everything but works well with fish and shellfish soups.

Leftover cooked vegetables have neither the flavor nor the nutritional content for making a good stock, but you can make beneficial use of some trimmings. Once again, beware of the cabbage family and avoid onion skins, which can make the stock bitter; however, the outer leaves of lettuce, broccoli, and cauliflower, mushroom stems, chard stems, and trimmings from asparagus spears and green beans will all add extra flavor—and at no extra cost. Sometimes the water in which vegetables have been cooked can be substituted for some of the water in the recipe—that from cooking asparagus, broccoli, cauliflower, chard, corn cobs, and green beans, for example.

The basic recipe can easily be adapted to make a brown stock, which has a deeper flavor and color and is especially suitable for meat soups. Substitute 2–3 large tomatoes for the potato, parsnips, and turnip. Cook the onion, leeks, celery, and carrots over very low heat, stirring occasionally, for about 30 minutes, until they are a rich golden brown. Meanwhile, broil the halved tomatoes until they are golden brown. Add the tomatoes in step 2 with the herbs.

Whatever vegetables you use for the stock and however you cook it, it is advisable not to season it with salt during cooking. As the stock becomes more concentrated, it can become unpleasantly salty. There is an even greater risk of this if you concentrate the stock even more later. Adding salt is best left until you make the soup. This also applies to the addition of spices.

For clarifying stock to make jewel-clear broths, see Jellied Vegetable Consommé (page 165).

Because stock can be stored in the freezer for up to 3 months, it is worth making a large batch. Freeze it in measured quantities, such as 2 cups, so it is easy to remove the amount you need to use for a particular soup.

So as the temperature drops outside in those long winter months, delicious and nutritious soups can be quickly and easily created for instant warmth. Whether you are entertaining guests, feeding the family, or need something tasty to serve at an impromptu gathering, soup wins every time—your only problem will be choosing which one to serve!

Basic Vegetable Stock

This is the recipe that all 100 variations of soup in the book are based on. For each recipe the basic stock is highlighted (✳) for easy reference, so then all you have to do is follow the easy steps each time and a world of delicious and delectable soups will await you.

Makes 4 cups

✳ 2 tbsp sunflower oil
✳ 1 onion, finely chopped
✳ 2 leeks, thinly sliced
✳ 2 celery stalks, finely chopped
✳ 1 large potato, diced
✳ 2 carrots, thinly sliced

✳ 2 small parsnips, thinly sliced
✳ 1 small turnip, thinly sliced
✳ 2 bay leaves
✳ 6 fresh parsley sprigs
✳ ⅔ cup dry white wine
✳ 4 cups water

1. Heat the oil in a large pan. Add the onion, leeks, celery, and potato and cook over a low heat, stirring frequently, for about 8 minutes, until softened and just beginning to color.

2. Add the carrots, parsnips, turnip, bay leaves, parsley sprigs, and white wine, stir well, and cook for 2 minutes, until the alcohol has evaporated. Increase the heat to medium, pour in the water, and bring to a boil. Reduce the heat, cover, and simmer for 1 hour.

3. Remove the pan from the heat and strain the basic vegetable stock into a bowl through a fine strainer, pressing the vegetables with the back of a ladle to extract as much liquid as possible; do not press the vegetables through the strainer. Strain again and let cool completely, then cover with plastic wrap, and store in the refrigerator for up to 2 days. Alternatively, freeze for up to 3 months.

Hearty

Summer Tomato Soup

1. Heat the olive oil in a large, heavy pan. Add the onion, scallions, garlic, and celery and cook over low heat, stirring occasionally, for 5 minutes, until softened. Add the tomatoes, cover, and simmer, stirring occasionally, for 50 minutes, until thickened.

2. Remove the pan from the heat and let cool slightly. Transfer the mixture to a food processor or blender, in batches if necessary, and process to a smooth puree, then pass the puree through a strainer into a clean pan.

3. Add the basic vegetable stock and bring to a boil, stirring constantly. Season to taste with cayenne, salt, and pepper, add the pasta, and bring back to a boil. Boil over medium heat for 8–10 minutes, until the pasta is tender, but still firm to the bite.

4. Meanwhile, make the garnish. Melt the butter in a small skillet. Add the parsley sprigs, in batches, and cook for a few seconds, then turn and cook for a few seconds more. Remove from the skillet and drain on paper towels.

5. Taste the soup and adjust the seasoning, if necessary. Ladle into warmed bowls, sprinkle with the fried parsley, and serve immediately.

Serves 6

3 tbsp olive oil

1 large onion, finely chopped

4 scallions, finely chopped

3 garlic cloves, finely chopped

2 celery stalks, finely chopped

1 lb 12 oz/800 g tomatoes, peeled and chopped

3 cups basic vegetable stock

pinch of cayenne pepper

¾ cup stellette or other small pasta shapes

salt and pepper

To garnish
6 tbsp sweet butter
12 fresh flat-leaf parsley sprigs

Tomato & White Bean Soup

1. Heat the olive oil in a large pan. Add the onions, celery, bell pepper, and garlic and cook over low heat, stirring occasionally, for 5 minutes, until softened.

2. Increase the heat to medium, add the tomatoes, and cook, stirring occasionally, for 5 minutes more, then pour in the basic vegetable stock. Stir in the tomato paste, sugar, and sweet paprika and season to taste with salt and pepper. Bring to a boil, reduce the heat, and simmer for 15 minutes.

3. Meanwhile, mash together the butter and flour to a paste in a small bowl with a fork. Stir the paste, in small pieces at a time, into the soup. Make sure each piece is fully incorporated before adding the next.

4. Add the beans, stir well, and simmer for another 5 minutes, until heated through. Sprinkle with the parsley and serve immediately.

Serves 6

3 tbsp olive oil

1⅔ cups chopped red onions

1 celery stalk with leaves, chopped

1 red bell pepper, seeded and chopped

2 garlic cloves, finely chopped

4 cups peeled and chopped plum tomatoes

✳ 5⅔ cups basic vegetable stock

2 tbsp tomato paste

1 tsp sugar

1 tbsp sweet paprika

1 tbsp butter

1 tbsp all-purpose flour

14 oz/400 g canned cannellini beans, drained and rinsed

salt and pepper

3 tbsp chopped fresh flat-leaf parsley, to garnish

Barley, Lentil & Onion Soup

1. Put the barley into a large pan, pour in the water, and bring to a boil. Reduce the heat, cover, and simmer gently, stirring frequently, for about 30 minutes, until all the liquid has been absorbed.

2. Add the basic vegetable stock, onions, lentils, ginger, and cumin and bring to a boil over medium heat. Reduce the heat, cover, and simmer, stirring occasionally, for 1½ hours, adding a little more stock if necessary.

3. Meanwhile, make the garnish. Spread out the onions on a thick layer of paper towels and cover with another thick layer. Let dry out for 30 minutes. Heat the oil in a skillet. Add the onions and cook over low heat, stirring constantly, for about 20 minutes, until well browned. Add the garlic and cook, stirring constantly, for 5 minutes more. Remove the onions with a slotted spoon and drain well on paper towels.

4. Season the soup to taste with salt and pepper, stir in the lemon juice and cilantro, and simmer for another 5 minutes. Serve immediately, garnished with the browned onions.

Serves 6

2 tbsp pearl barley

⅔ cup water

⁎ 7½ cups basic vegetable stock

1 lb 2 oz/500 g onions, thinly sliced into rings

⅔ cup Puy lentils

½ tsp ground ginger

1 tsp ground cumin

3 tablespoons lemon juice

2 tbsp chopped fresh cilantro

salt and pepper

To garnish

2 onions, halved and thinly sliced

5 tbsp vegetable oil

2 garlic cloves, finely chopped

Green Vegetable Soup

1. Pour the basic vegetable stock into a pan and bring to a boil. Meanwhile, heat the oil in a large pan. Add the leeks and cook over low heat, stirring occasionally, for 5 minutes, until softened, then remove the pan from the heat.

2. Stir in the flour until fully incorporated, then gradually stir in the hot stock, a little at a time. Season with salt and pepper and add the thyme and fennel seeds.

3. Return the pan to the heat and bring to a boil, stirring constantly. Add the lettuce, spinach, peas, watercress, and mint and bring back to a boil. Boil, stirring constantly, for 3–4 minutes, then reduce the heat, cover, and simmer gently for 30 minutes.

4. Remove the soup from the heat and let cool slightly. Ladle it into a food processor or blender, in batches if necessary, and process to a smooth puree. Return the soup to the rinsed-out pan and reheat, stirring occasionally. When it is piping hot, ladle into warmed bowls, sprinkle with the parsley, and serve with garlic and herb bread.

Serves 6

- generous 6¾ cups basic vegetable stock
- 3 tablespoons olive oil
- 2 leeks, white parts only, chopped
- 2 tbsp all-purpose flour
- 1 tsp dried thyme
- ½ tsp fennel seeds
- 1 Boston lettuce, coarsely chopped
- 1 lb 2 oz/500 g spinach, coarse stalks removed
- 2½ cups shelled fresh or frozen peas
- 1 bunch of watercress or arugula
- 4 tbsp chopped fresh mint
- salt and pepper
- 2 tbsp chopped fresh parsley, to garnish
- garlic and herb bread, to serve

5

Squash & Lentil Soup

1. Heat the oil in a large pan. Add the onions and garlic and cook over low heat, stirring occasionally, for 5 minutes, until softened. Add the cumin, cinnamon, nutmeg, ginger, and coriander and cook, stirring constantly, for 1 minute.

2. Stir in the butternut squash and lentils and cook, stirring constantly for 2 minutes, then pour in the basic vegetable stock, and bring to a boil over medium heat. Reduce the heat and simmer, stirring occasionally, for 50–60 minutes, until the vegetables are tender.

3. Remove from the heat and let cool slightly, then ladle into a food processor or blender, in batches if necessary, and process to a smooth puree.

4. Return the soup to the rinsed-out pan, stir in the lemon juice, season to taste with salt and pepper, and reheat gently. Ladle into warmed bowls, top with a swirl of crème fraîche, and serve.

Serves 6

3 tbsp olive oil

2 large onions, chopped

2 garlic cloves, chopped

2 tsp ground cumin

1 tsp ground cinnamon

½ tsp freshly grated nutmeg

½ tsp ground ginger

½ tsp ground coriander

2 lb 4 oz/1 kg butternut squash or pumpkin, seeded, and cut into small chunks

1½ cups red or yellow lentils

7½ cups basic vegetable stock

3 tbsp lemon juice

salt and pepper

crème fraîche or strained plain yogurt, to garnish

Ribollita

1. Put half the beans into a food processor and process briefly to a coarse puree. Scrape into a bowl and set aside.

2. Heat the oil in a large pan. Add the onion, leek, garlic, carrots, and celery and cook over low heat, stirring occasionally, for 8–10 minutes. Add the potatoes and zucchini and cook, stirring constantly, for 2 minutes.

3. Add the tomatoes, tomato paste, and dried chile, if using, and cook, stirring constantly, for 3 minutes, then stir in the bean puree. Cook, stirring constantly, for 2 minutes more.

4. Pour in the basic vegetable stock and add the black cabbage and savoy cabbage. Bring to a boil, reduce the heat, and simmer for 2 hours.

5. Meanwhile, preheat the broiler. Rub the bread with the halved garlic cloves and toast on both sides.

6. Stir the whole beans into the soup and heat through gently for 10 minutes. Season with salt and pepper. Put the garlic-flavored bread in the base of warmed soup bowls and ladle the soup over it. Drizzle with a little oil and serve immediately.

Serves 6

14 oz/400 g canned cannellini beans, drained and rinsed

3 tbsp olive oil, plus extra for drizzling

1 Bermuda onion, chopped

1 leek, chopped

4 garlic cloves, finely chopped

2 carrots, diced

2 celery stalks, chopped

2 potatoes, diced

2 zucchini, diced

2 large tomatoes, peeled, seeded, and chopped

1 tsp sun-dried tomato paste

1 dried chile, crushed (optional)

7½ cups basic vegetable stock

2½ cups shredded black cabbage, kale, or Swiss chard

2½ cups shredded savoy cabbage

6 slices of ciabatta

2 garlic cloves, halved

salt and pepper

Bacon & Potato Soup

1. Heat the olive oil in a large pan. Add the bacon, onions, and garlic and cook over medium heat, stirring frequently, for 5–7 minutes, until the bacon is crisp and the onions are lightly browned.

2. Pour in the basic vegetable stock and add the potatoes, cabbage, Worcestershire sauce, and mustard, season with pepper to taste, and mix well. Bring to a boil, then reduce the heat and simmer, stirring occasionally, for 30 minutes.

3. Remove the pan from the heat and let cool slightly, then transfer 2½ cups to a food processor or blender. Process briefly to a coarse puree and return to the pan. Stir well and return the soup to the heat. Cook, stirring frequently, for 5–10 minutes, until heated through. Season with salt to taste, stir in the parsley, and ladle into warmed bowls. Serve immediately with crusty rolls.

Serves 6

2 tbsp olive oil

1 cup chopped lean bacon

2 onions, chopped

2 garlic cloves, finely chopped

7½ cups basic vegetable stock

2⅓ cups diced potatoes

3 cups shredded savoy cabbage

1 teaspoon Worcestershire or Tabasco sauce

1 tsp Dijon mustard

3 tbsp finely chopped fresh flat-leaf parsley

salt and pepper

crusty rolls, to serve

Pork Soup with Bulgur Wheat

1. Heat the oil in a large pan. Add the pork, onions, and garlic, if using, and cook over medium heat, stirring occasionally, for 8 minutes, until the meat is lightly browned.

2. Pour in the wine and cook, stirring constantly, for 2 minutes, until the alcohol has evaporated, then pour in the basic vegetable stock. Reduce the heat, cover, and simmer for 15 minutes.

3. Add the bulgur wheat, season with salt and pepper, and cook for 15 minutes more, until the meat and wheat are tender and the soup has thickened.

4. Stir in the lemon juice. Taste and adjust the seasoning, if necessary. Serve the soup immediately, sprinkled with a little cayenne pepper and accompanied by soda bread and butter.

Serves 4–6

5 tablespoons olive oil

1 lb 2 oz/500 g boneless pork, diced

2 onions, chopped

2 garlic cloves, finely chopped (optional)

½ cup white wine

6¼ cups basic vegetable stock

generous 1 cup bulgur wheat

3 tablespoons lemon juice

pinch of cayenne pepper

salt and pepper

soda bread and butter, to serve

Salt Pork & Lentil Soup

1. Put the salt pork into a large pan and cook over medium heat, stirring frequently, for 8–10 minutes, until it has released most of its fat and is browned all over. Remove from the pan with a slotted spoon and drain on paper towels. Set aside.

2. Add the oil to the pan and heat. Add the onion, garlic, and potatoes and cook over low heat, stirring occasionally, for 5 minutes, until the onion has softened. Stir in the lentils and cook, stirring constantly, for 5 minutes,.

3. Pour in the basic vegetable stock, increase the heat to medium, add the bouquet garni, and bring to a boil, stirring constantly. Reduce the heat, cover, and simmer for 1½–2 hours, until the lentils are very soft. Stir in the salt pork, season with salt and pepper, if necessary, and cook, stirring occasionally, for another 10 minutes, until heated through.

4. Remove the pan from the heat. Remove and discard the bouquet garni. Pour the soup into a warmed tureen and serve immediately with crusty bread.

Serves 6–8

8 oz/225 g salt pork, diced

2 tbsp olive oil

1 onion, chopped

3 garlic cloves, finely chopped

4 potatoes, diced

2¼ cups red lentils

8¾ cups basic vegetable stock

1 bouquet garni (1 bay leaf,
   1 fresh thyme sprig, and
   3 fresh parsley sprigs,
   tied together)

salt and pepper

crusty bread, to serve

10

Mixed Vegetable Soup with Lamb Meatballs

1. Put the onions, celeriac, rutabaga, carrots, potatoes, bell peppers, tomatoes, peas, and lemon slices into a large pan, pour in the basic vegetable stock, and season with salt and pepper. Bring to a boil, then reduce the heat, cover, and simmer for 25–30 minutes.

2. Meanwhile, make the meatballs. Combine the lamb, parsley, and rice in a bowl, kneading well until thoroughly mixed. Season with salt and pepper. Break off pieces of the mixture, about the size of golf balls, and shape them into balls between the palms of your hand. Dust with flour, shaking off the excess.

3. Add the meatballs to the soup, re-cover the pan, and cook, stirring occasionally, for 40–45 minutes more. Serve immediately.

Serves 6

2 onions, finely chopped

1 small celeriac, diced

½ rutabaga, diced

3 carrots, diced

2 potatoes, diced

2 red bell peppers, seeded and diced

4 tomatoes, peeled, seeded, and chopped

1 cup shelled fresh or frozen peas

1 lemon, sliced

✳ generous 6¾ cups basic vegetable stock

salt and pepper

Lamb meatballs

12 oz/350 g ground lamb

3 tbsp chopped fresh flat-leaf parsley

⅓ cup medium-grain rice

all-purpose flour, for dusting

salt and pepper

Beef Noodle Soup

1. Put the dried mushrooms into a bowl, pour in boiling water to cover, and let soak for 20 minutes. If using Chinese mushrooms, drain and rinse. If using porcini, drain, reserving the soaking water. Strain the soaking water through a fine strainer or coffee filter paper into a bowl.

2. Heat the oil in a large pan. Add the strips of beef and cook, stirring constantly, until browned all over. Remove with a slotted spoon and drain on paper towels.

3. Add the carrots, scallions, garlic, and ginger to the pan and cook, stirring constantly, for 5 minutes. Return the beef to the pan, pour in the basic vegetable stock, and add the soy sauce, hoisin sauce, and rice wine. Add the mushrooms and porcini soaking water, if using. Season with pepper and bring to a boil over medium heat, then reduce the heat and simmer for 15 minutes.

4. Add the noodles and spinach to the pan, stir well, and simmer for another 7–8 minutes. Taste and add more pepper or soy sauce, if necessary. Serve immediately.

Serves 6

¼ cup dried Chinese mushrooms or porcini mushrooms

3 tbsp corn oil

1 lb 2 oz/500 g lean beef, such as tenderloin or sirloin, cut into thin strips

3 medium carrots, cut into julienne strips

10 scallions, finely shredded

2 garlic cloves, finely chopped

1 tbsp finely chopped fresh ginger

7½ cups basic vegetable stock

4 tbsp dark soy sauce

1 tbsp hoisin sauce

6 tbsp Chinese rice wine or dry sherry

5 oz/140 g egg noodles

1⅔ cups shredded spinach leaves

pepper

Split Pea & Sausage Soup

1. Put the pork into a large pan and pour in the basic vegetable stock. Add the onion, leeks, carrots, celery, apple, peas, bouquet garni, and molasses and bring to a boil. Using a skimmer or slotted spoon, skim off any foam that rises to the surface, then reduce the heat, cover, and simmer, stirring occasionally, for 2 hours.

2. Season the soup to taste with salt and pepper and remove and discard the bouquet garni. Stir in the sausages and butter and simmer for another 5 minutes. Serve immediately with rye bread.

Serves 6

6 oz/175 g boneless side of pork, cut into cubes

8¾ cups basic vegetable stock

1 onion, chopped

4 leeks, chopped

3 carrots, chopped

3 celery stalks, chopped

1 tart apple, peeled, cored, and chopped

1⅔ cups split peas, soaked overnight in cold water to cover, drained and rinsed

1 bouquet garni (2 fresh parsley sprigs, 1 fresh thyme sprig, and 1 fresh mint sprig)

1 tbsp molasses

4 bockwurst, Wienerwurst, or frankfurters, cut into 1-inch/2.5-cm lengths

2 tbsp butter

salt and pepper

crusty rye bread, to serve

Sauerkraut & Sausage Soup

1. Melt the butter in a large pan over low heat. Add the all-purpose flour and paprika and cook, stirring constantly, for 2 minutes, then remove the pan from the heat. Gradually stir in the basic vegetable stock, a little at a time, until fully incorporated and the mixture is smooth.

2. Return the pan to medium heat and bring to a boil, stirring constantly. Add the sauerkraut and sausages and season with salt and pepper. Reduce the heat, cover, and simmer for 30 minutes.

3. Meanwhile, make the dumplings. Sift together the flour and salt into a bowl. Beat the egg in another bowl, then gradually beat in the dry ingredients, a little at a time. Turn out onto a floured surface and knead until smooth. Cover and let rest for 15 minutes.

4. Divide the dough into 6 pieces and roll into sausage shapes. Flour your hands, pinch off pieces of the dough, and add to the soup. Re-cover the pan and simmer for 5 minutes more. Remove the pan from the heat, stir in the sour cream, and serve immediately.

Serves 6

2 tbsp butter

1 tbsp all-purpose flour

1 tbsp sweet paprika

8¾ cups basic vegetable stock

1 lb 7 oz/650 g sauerkraut, drained

1 lb 2 oz/500 g smoked pork sausages, cut into 1-inch/2.5-cm slices

⅔ cup sour cream

salt and pepper

Dumplings

¾ cup white bread flour, plus extra for dusting

pinch of salt

1 extra large egg

Chicken & Lentil Soup

1. Heat the oil in a large pan. Add the onion, leeks, carrots, celery, and mushrooms and cook over low heat, stirring occasionally, for 5–7 minutes, until softened but not colored.

2. Increase the heat to medium, pour in the wine, and cook for 2–3 minutes, until the alcohol has evaporated, then pour in the basic vegetable stock. Bring to a boil, add the bay leaf and herbs, reduce the heat, cover, and simmer for 30 minutes.

3. Add the lentils, re-cover the pan, and simmer, stirring occasionally, for 40 minutes more, until they are tender.

4. Stir in the chicken, season to taste with salt and pepper, and simmer for another 5–10 minutes, until heated through. Serve immediately.

Serves 6

3 tbsp olive oil

1 large onion, chopped

2 leeks, chopped

2 carrots, chopped

2 celery stalks, chopped

scant 2½ cups chopped white mushrooms

4 tbsp dry white wine

5 cups basic vegetable stock

1 bay leaf

2 tsp dried mixed herbs

¾ cup Puy lentils

scant 2½ cups diced cooked chicken

salt and pepper

15

Chicken Soup with Matzo Balls

1. First, make the matzo balls. Melt 1 tbsp of the butter in a small skillet. Add the grated onion and cook over low heat, stirring occasionally, for 5 minutes, until softened. Remove from the heat and let cool.

2. Beat the remaining butter in a bowl until fluffy, then gradually beat in the egg and egg yolk. Add the parsley and onion, season with salt and pepper, and mix well, then beat in the water. Mix in the matzo crumbs until thoroughly incorporated. Cover and let rest in the refrigerator for 30 minutes.

3. Meanwhile, put the chicken into a large pan and pour in the basic vegetable stock. Bring to a boil over a medium–low heat, skimming off the foam that rises to the surface. Simmer for 15 minutes.

4. Add the chopped onion, celery, carrots, tomatoes, and parsley and season with salt and pepper. Reduce the heat, cover, and simmer for 50–60 minutes, until the chicken is cooked through and tender. Meanwhile, shape the matzo mixture into 18 balls.

5. Strain the soup into a clean pan, reserving the chicken quarters. Remove and discard the skin and bones and cut the meat into bite-size pieces. Add the chicken, vermicelli, and matzo balls to the pan, cover, and simmer gently for 20–30 minutes. Serve immediately.

Serves 6

2 chicken quarters
11¼ cups basic vegetable stock
2 onions, chopped
2 celery stalks, chopped
2 carrots, chopped
2 tomatoes, peeled and chopped
2 fresh parsley sprigs
2 oz/55 g vermicelli
salt and pepper

Matzo balls
4 tbsp butter
½ onion, grated
1 egg
1 egg yolk
1 tbsp finely chopped fresh parsley
1 tbsp water
2 cups crushed matzo crackers
salt and pepper

Chicken & Almond Soup

1. Melt the butter in a pan. Add the leeks and ginger and cook over low heat, stirring occasionally, for 5 minutes, until softened. Add the chicken, carrots, peas, chiles, and ground almonds and cook, stirring constantly, for 10 minutes.

2. Stir in the cilantro, remove from the heat, and let cool slightly. Spoon the chicken mixture into a food processor and process until very finely chopped. Add the basic vegetable stock and process to a puree.

3. Return the mixture to the pan, season with salt and pepper, and bring to a boil. Reduce the heat to very low and gradually stir in the cream; do not let the soup boil. Simmer, stirring frequently, for 2 minutes. Ladle into warmed bowls, sprinkle with chopped cilantro and ground almonds, and serve.

Serves 6

½ cup butter

2 leeks, chopped

1½ tbsp finely chopped fresh ginger

6 oz/175 g skinless, boneless chicken, diced

2 carrots, chopped

¾ cup shelled fresh or frozen peas

2 green chiles, seeded and chopped

1¼ cups ground almonds, plus extra to decorate

1 tbsp chopped fresh cilantro, plus extra to garnish

generous 3 cups basic vegetable stock

1½ cups light cream

salt and pepper

17

Chicken Soup with Leeks & Rice

1. Heat the oil in a pan. Add the leeks and cook over low heat, stirring occasionally, for 5 minutes, until softened. Add the chicken, increase the heat to medium, and cook, stirring frequently, for 2 minutes. Add the rice and cook, stirring constantly, for 2 minutes more.

2. Pour in the basic vegetable stock, add the Worcestershire sauce and chives, and bring to a boil. Reduce the heat, cover, and simmer for 20–25 minutes.

3. Meanwhile, preheat the broiler. Broil the bacon for 2–4 minutes on each side, until crisp. Remove and let cool, then crumble.

4. Season the soup to taste with salt and pepper and stir in the parsley. Ladle into warmed bowls, sprinkle with the crumbled bacon, and serve.

Serves 6

2 tbsp olive oil

3 leeks, chopped

6 skinless, boneless chicken thighs, diced

generous ¼ cup long-grain rice

5⅔ cups basic vegetable stock

dash of Worcestershire sauce

6 fresh chives, chopped

6 thin bacon slices

2 tbsp chopped fresh flat-leaf parsley

salt and pepper

Fish Soup with Semolina & Dill Dumplings

1. Put the chorizo into a heavy pan and cook over medium–low heat, stirring frequently, for 5 minutes until lightly browned. Add the fish and cook, occasionally stirring gently, for 2 minutes.

2. Sprinkle in the paprika and cayenne, pour in the basic vegetable stock, and bring to a boil. Reduce the heat, cover, and simmer for 10 minutes.

3. Add the potatoes, tomatoes, and parsley, stir gently, re-cover the pan, and simmer for 10 minutes.

4. Meanwhile, make the semolina and dill dumplings. Combine the semolina, salt, and dill in a bowl. Lightly beat together the egg and milk in another bowl, then stir into the dry ingredients until thoroughly combined. Cover and let rest in the refrigerator for 10 minutes.

5. Scoop up tablespoonfuls of the dumpling mixture and add them to the soup. Season to taste with salt and pepper. Re-cover the pan and simmer for another 10 minutes. Serve immediately.

Serves 6

¾ cup diced chorizo

1 lb 2 oz/500 g white fish fillets, skinned and diced

1 tbsp sweet paprika

pinch of cayenne pepper

6¼ cups basic vegetable stock

4 potatoes, diced

4 tomatoes, peeled and diced

1 tbsp chopped fresh flat-leaf parsley

salt and pepper

Semolina and dill dumplings

½ cup fine semolina

pinch of salt

1 tbsp chopped fresh dill

1 egg

3 tbsp milk

Fish & Sweet Potato Soup

1. Put the fish, sweet potato, onion, carrots, and cinnamon into a pan, pour in 4 cups of the basic vegetable stock, and bring to a boil. Reduce the heat, cover, and simmer for 30 minutes.

2. Meanwhile, scrub the clams under cold running water and remove any with broken shells or that do not shut immediately when sharply tapped. Put them into a pan, pour in the wine, cover, and cook over high heat, shaking the pan occasionally, for 3–5 minutes, until the clams have opened. Remove from the heat and lift out the clams with a slotted spoon, reserving the cooking liquid. Discard any clams that remain shut. Strain the cooking liquid through a fine strainer into a bowl.

3. Remove the pan of fish and vegetables from the heat and let cool slightly, then ladle the mixture into a food processor, in batches if necessary, and process until smooth.

4. Return the soup to the pan, add the remaining stock and the reserved cooking liquid, and bring back to a boil. Reduce the heat and gradually stir in the cream; do not let the soup boil. Add the clams, season to taste with salt and pepper, and simmer, stirring frequently, for 2 minutes, until heated through. Garnish with parsley, drizzle with olive oil, and serve immediately.

Serves 6

12 oz/350 g white fish fillet, skinned

scant 1 cup diced sweet potato

1 onion, chopped

2 carrots, diced

½ tsp ground cinnamon

7½ cups basic vegetable stock

14 oz/400 g clams

⅔ cup dry white wine

1 cup light cream

salt and pepper

chopped fresh flat-leaf parsley, to garnish

extra virgin olive oil, for drizzling

20

Clam & Pasta Soup

1. Heat the oil in a large pan. Add the onion and garlic and cook over low heat, stirring occasionally, for 5 minutes, until softened. Add the tomatoes, tomato paste, sugar, oregano, and basic vegetable stock and season with salt and pepper. Mix well and bring to a boil, then reduce the heat, cover, and simmer, stirring occasionally, for 10 minutes.

2. Meanwhile, scrub the clams under cold running water and discard any with broken shells or that do not shut immediately when sharply tapped. Put the clams into a pan, pour in the wine, cover, and cook over high heat, shaking the pan occasionally, for 3–5 minutes, until the clams have opened. Remove from the heat and lift out the clams with a slotted spoon, reserving the cooking liquid. Discard any clams that remain shut and remove the remainder from the half shells. Strain the reserved cooking liquid through a fine strainer into a bowl.

3. Add the pasta to the soup and simmer, uncovered, for 10 minutes. Add the clams and the reserved cooking liquid, stir well, and heat gently for 4–5 minutes; do not let the soup come back to a boil. If the soup is very thick, add a little hot water or stock. Taste and adjust the seasoning, if necessary, stir in the parsley, and serve immediately.

Serves 6

3 tbsp olive oil

1 Bermuda onion, finely chopped

3 garlic cloves, finely chopped

1 lb 5 oz/600 g canned chopped tomatoes

2 tbsp tomato paste

2 tsp sugar

1 tsp dried oregano

4 cups basic vegetable stock

1 lb 2 oz/500 g clams

¾ cup dry white wine

¾ cup conchigliette or other small pasta shapes

3 tbsp chopped fresh flat-leaf parsley

salt and pepper

Quick Sea Scallop Soup with Pasta

1. Slice the sea scallops in half horizontally and season with salt and pepper.

2. Pour the milk and basic vegetable stock into a pan, add a pinch of salt, and bring to a boil. Add the peas and pasta, bring back to a boil, and cook for 8–10 minutes, until the taglialini is tender but still firm to the bite.

3. Meanwhile, melt the butter in a skillet. Add the scallions and cook over low heat, stirring occasionally, for 3 minutes. Add the sea scallops and cook for 45 seconds on each side. Pour in the wine, add the prosciutto, and cook for 2–3 minutes.

4. Stir the sea scallop mixture into the soup, taste, and adjust the seasoning, if necessary, and garnish with the parsley. Serve immediately.

Serves 6

1 lb 2 oz/500 g shelled sea scallops

1½ cups milk

generous 6¾ cups basic vegetable stock

generous 1 cup frozen baby peas

6 oz/175 g taglialini

5 tbsp butter

2 scallions, finely chopped

¾ cup dry white wine

3 slices of prosciutto, cut into thin strips

salt and pepper

chopped fresh flat-leaf parsley, to garnish

22

Mediterranean Fish Soup with Garlic Mayonnaise

1. Cut out and discard the gills of any reserved fish heads. Cut the fish fillets into chunks. Put the fish bones, heads, and trimmings into a pan, pour in the wine vinegar, half the lemon juice, and the basic vegetable stock, add the herbes de Provence and bay leaves, and bring to a boil. Season with salt, reduce the heat, and simmer for 30 minutes.

2. Meanwhile, make the garlic mayonnaise. Pound the garlic with a pinch of salt in a mortar with a pestle. Transfer to a bowl, add the egg yolks, and whisk briefly with an electric mixer until creamy. Combine the oils in a pitcher and, whisking constantly, gradually add them to the egg mixture. When about half the oil has been incorporated, add the remainder in a thin, steady stream, whisking constantly. Stir in lemon juice to thin to the desired consistency. Transfer the mayonnaise to a sauce boat, cover, and set aside.

3. Strain the cooking liquid into a bowl and discard the contents of the strainer. Measure the cooking liquid and make up to 7½ cups with water, if necessary. Return it to the pan.

4. Beat the egg yolks with the remaining lemon juice in a bowl and stir it into the pan. Add the pieces of fish, stir gently to mix, and cook over low heat for 7–8 minutes, until the fish is tender and the soup has thickened. Do not let the soup boil.

5. Remove the pan from the heat and pour the soup into a warmed tureen. Serve immediately, handing the garlic mayonnaise separately and accompanied by toasted bread.

Serves 6

4 lb 8 oz/2 kg mixed white fish, such as gurnard, red snapper, grouper, and haddock, filleted, with bones, heads, and trimmings reserved

2 tbsp white wine vinegar

2 tbsp lemon juice

7½ cups basic vegetable stock

2 tsp herbes de Provence

2 bay leaves

4 egg yolks

salt and pepper

toasted country bread, to serve

Garlic mayonnaise

4 garlic cloves

2 egg yolks

½ cup extra virgin olive oil

½ cup sunflower or safflower oil

1–2 tbsp lemon juice

salt

Tasty

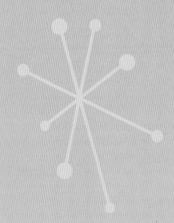

23

Carrot & Parsnip Soup

1. Put the carrots, parsnips, shallots, and chervil into a pan, pour in the basic vegetable stock, and season with salt and pepper. Bring to a boil, reduce the heat, and simmer for 20–25 minutes, until the vegetables are tender.

2. Remove the pan from the heat and let cool slightly. Remove and discard the chervil, then transfer to a food processor or blender, in batches if necessary, and process to a puree.

3. Return the soup to the rinsed-out pan and reheat gently. Ladle into warmed bowls, swirl about 1 tablespoon cream on the top of each, and serve.

Serves 6

1¾ cups chopped carrots
1¾ cups chopped parsnips
4 shallots, chopped
4 fresh chervil sprigs
3¾ cups basic vegetable stock
salt and pepper
heavy cream, to garnish

24

Carrot & Cilantro Soup

1. Heat the oil in a large pan. Add the onion and cook over low heat, stirring occasionally, for 5 minutes, until softened.

2. Add the potato and celery and cook, stirring occasionally, for another 5 minutes, then add the carrots, and cook, stirring occasionally, for 5 minutes more. Cover the pan, reduce the heat to very low, and cook, shaking the pan occasionally, for 10 minutes.

3. Pour in the basic vegetable stock and bring to a boil, then cover, and simmer for 10 minutes, until the vegetables are tender.

4. Meanwhile, melt the butter in a skillet. Add the coriander seeds and cook, stirring constantly, for 1 minute. Add the chopped cilantro and cook, stirring constantly, for 1 minute, then remove from the heat.

5. Remove the soup from the heat and let cool slightly. Transfer to a food processor or blender, in batches if necessary, and process to a puree. Return the soup to the rinsed-out pan, stir in the cilantro mixture and milk and season to taste with salt and pepper. Reheat gently, then serve, sprinkled with chopped cilantro.

Serves 6

3 tbsp olive oil

1 red onion, chopped

1 large potato, chopped

1 celery stalk, chopped

2¾ cups chopped carrots

4 cups basic vegetable stock

1 tbsp butter

2 tsp coriander seeds, crushed

1½ tbsp chopped fresh cilantro, plus extra to garnish

1 cup milk

salt and pepper

Cream of Tomato Soup

1. Melt the butter in a large pan. Add the onion and cook over low heat, stirring occasionally, for 5 minutes, until softened. Add the tomatoes, bay leaf, basil, and parsley, season with salt and pepper, and simmer, stirring occasionally, for 15 minutes, until the tomatoes have cooked down and most of the liquid has evaporated.

2. Increase the heat to medium, pour in the basic vegetable stock, and bring to a boil. Reduce the heat, cover, and simmer for 25 minutes.

3. Meanwhile, make the croutons. Cut the bread into ¼-inch/5-mm squares. Heat the oil in a skillet. Add the bread squares and cook, turning and tossing frequently, until golden brown all over. Remove with a slotted spoon and drain on paper towels.

4. Remove the soup from the heat and let cool slightly. Remove and discard the herbs and stir the ketchup into the soup. Transfer the soup to a food processor or blender, in batches if necessary, and process to a puree. If any tomato seeds remain, pass the puree through a fine strainer.

5. Return the soup to the rinsed-out pan and reheat. Stir in the cream and heat gently for 1–2 minutes more, until the soup is hot. Taste and adjust the seasoning, if necessary, and ladle into warmed bowls. Tear the basil leaves and sprinkle them over the soup, add the croutons, and serve immediately.

Serves 6

4 tbsp butter

1 onion, chopped

2 lb 4 oz/1 kg ripe tomatoes, peeled, seeded, and chopped

1 bay leaf

4 fresh basil sprigs

4 fresh parsley sprigs

7½ cups basic vegetable stock

1 tbsp ketchup

¾ cup heavy cream

salt and pepper

fresh basil leaves, to garnish

Croutons
2 slices day-old bread, crusts removed

2 tbsp olive oil

Tomato & Parsnip Soup

1. Melt the butter in a pan. Add the onions and garlic and cook over low heat, stirring occasionally, for 5 minutes, until softened. Add the parsnips and cook, stirring occasionally, for 5 minutes more.

2. Sprinkle in the flour and thyme, season with salt and pepper, and cook, stirring constantly, for 2 minutes. Remove the pan from the heat. Gradually stir in the basic vegetable stock, a little at a time, then stir in the milk and add the bay leaf and tomatoes.

3. Return the pan to medium heat and bring to a boil, stirring constantly. Reduce the heat, cover, and simmer for 45 minutes, until the parsnips are tender.

4. Remove the pan from the heat and let cool slightly. Remove and discard the bay leaf. Transfer the soup to a food processor or blender, in batches if necessary, and process to a puree.

5. Return the soup to the rinsed-out pan and reheat gently, stirring occasionally. Taste and adjust the seasoning, if necessary. Ladle into warmed bowls, garnish with snipped chives, and serve immediately.

Serves 6

2 tbsp butter

2 onions, chopped

1 garlic clove, finely chopped

2¾ cups chopped parsnips

3 tbsp all-purpose flour

½ tsp dried thyme

4 cups basic vegetable stock

⅔ cup milk

1 bay leaf

14 oz/400 g canned chopped tomatoes

salt and pepper

snipped fresh chives, to garnish

27

Mushroom Soup

1. Tear the bread into pieces and put it into a bowl. Pour in cold water to cover and let soak for 10 minutes, then drain, and squeeze out.

2. Meanwhile, melt the butter in a large pan. Add the onion and cook over low heat, stirring occasionally, for 8–10 minutes, until golden. Add the mushrooms and garlic and cook, stirring frequently, for 5–7 minutes, until they have released their liquid.

3. Add the bread and thyme and pour in the wine. Cook for 2 minutes, until the alcohol has evaporated, then pour in the basic vegetable stock and bring to a boil over medium heat. Reduce the heat, cover, and simmer for 20–25 minutes.

4. Remove the pan from the heat and let cool slightly. Transfer the soup to a food processor or blender, in batches if necessary, and process to a puree.

5. Return the soup to the rinsed-out pan, season to taste with salt and pepper, and reheat gently, stirring occasionally. Ladle into warmed bowls and serve.

Serves 6

5 oz/140 g ciabatta or other rustic bread, crusts removed

4 tbsp butter

1 small onion, chopped

8½ cups coarsely chopped portobello mushrooms

1 garlic clove, finely chopped

½ tsp dried thyme

⅔ cup red wine or Madeira

4 cups basic vegetable stock

salt and pepper

Mushroom & Ginger Soup

1. Heat the oil in a pan. Add the shallots and ginger and cook over low heat, stirring occasionally, for 5 minutes, until softened. Add the mushrooms and cook, stirring frequently, for 5–7 minutes, until they have released their liquid.

2. Pour in the basic vegetable stock and bring to a boil. Reduce the heat and simmer for 10 minutes.

3. Remove the pan from the heat and let cool slightly. Transfer the soup to a food processor or blender, in batches if necessary, and process to a puree.

4. Return to the rinsed out-pan, stir in the sour cream, season to taste with salt and pepper, and reheat gently, stirring occasionally. Ladle into warmed bowls, sprinkle with the parsley, and serve immediately.

Serves 6

3 tbsp olive oil

4 shallots, chopped

1 tbsp finely chopped fresh ginger

2 lb 4 oz/1 kg cremini mushrooms, coarsely chopped

4 cups basic vegetable stock

⅔ cup sour cream

2 tbsp chopped fresh flat-leaf parsley, to garnish

salt and pepper

Red Bell Pepper Soup

1. Preheat the broiler. Put the bell peppers on a cookie sheet and broil, turning frequently, for 10 minutes, until blistered and charred. Remove with tongs, put them into a plastic bag, seal the top, and let stand until cool enough to handle. Peel, halve, and seed them, then chop the flesh.

2. Meanwhile, pour the basic vegetable stock into a pan and bring to a boil. Add the bell peppers, onion, carrots, cucumber, and cauliflower and bring back to a boil. Reduce the heat, cover, and simmer for 20 minutes.

3. Remove the pan from the heat and let cool slightly. Transfer the soup to a food processor blender, in batches if necessary, and process to a puree.

4. Return the soup to the rinsed-out pan. Beat together the egg yolk and cream in a bowl and stir into the soup, season to taste with salt and pepper, and reheat gently, stirring occasionally; do not let the soup boil. Stir in the sherry, ladle into warmed bowls, and serve immediately.

Serves 6

2 red bell peppers

5⅔ cups basic vegetable stock

1 Bermuda onion, finely chopped

2 carrots, chopped

¾ cup peeled, seeded, and chopped cucumber

scant 1 cup cauliflower florets

1 extra large egg yolk

6 tbsp heavy cream

3 tbsp dry sherry

salt and pepper

Cauliflower & Coconut Soup

1. Pour the basic vegetable stock into a pan and add the lemongrass, lime rind, and galangal. Pound 1 garlic clove with the cilantro roots in a mortar with a pestle and add to the pan. Bring to a boil, then reduce the heat, cover, and simmer for 40 minutes. Meanwhile, finely chop the remaining garlic.

2. Remove the pan from the heat and strain the stock into a bowl. Discard the contents of the strainer.

3. Heat the oil in a pan. Add the scallions, chiles, and chopped garlic and cook over low heat, stirring occasionally, for 5 minutes. Add the cauliflower and cook, stirring frequently, for 6–8 minutes, until just beginning to color.

4. Add the strained stock, coconut milk, Thai fish sauce, if using, and chopped cilantro and bring to a boil over medium heat. Stir well, reduce the heat, cover, and simmer for 25–30 minutes. Season to taste with salt and pepper and stir in the lime juice. Ladle into warmed bowls, garnish with cilantro and browned onions, and serve immediately.

Serves 6

5⅔ cups basic vegetable stock

2 lemongrass stalks, bruised

coarsely grated rind of 1 lime

6 slices of galangal or fresh ginger

2 garlic cloves

6 cilantro roots

3 tbsp peanut oil

6 scallions, thinly sliced

1 green chile, seeded and chopped

1 red Thai chile, seeded and thinly sliced

1 large cauliflower, cut into small florets

1¾ cups canned coconut milk

2 tbsp Thai fish sauce (optional)

2 tbsp chopped fresh cilantro, plus extra to garnish

1 tbsp lime juice

salt and pepper

browned onions, to garnish (see page 19)

Jerusalem Artichoke Soup

1. Fill a bowl with water and stir in the lemon juice. Peel the artichokes and cut into chunks, then immediately drop them into the bowl of acidulated water to prevent discoloration.

2. Heat the butter with the oil in a large pan. Add the onion and cook over low heat, stirring occasionally, for 5 minutes, until softened. Drain the artichokes, add them to the pan, and stir well. Cover and cook, stirring occasionally, for 15 minutes.

3. Pour in the basic vegetable stock and milk, increase the heat to medium, and bring to a boil. Reduce the heat, re-cover the pan, and simmer for 20 minutes, until the artichokes are soft.

4. Remove the pan from the heat and let cool slightly. Add the chives and transfer the soup to a food processor or blender, in batches if necessary, and process to a puree.

5. Pour the soup back into the rinsed-out pan, stir in the cream, and season with salt and pepper. Reheat gently, stirring occasionally, but do not let the soup boil. Ladle into warmed bowls, garnish with croutons, drizzle over the oil, and serve immediately.

Serves 6

1 tbsp lemon juice

1 lb 9 oz/700 g Jerusalem artichokes

4 tbsp butter

1 tbsp sunflower oil

1 large onion, chopped

5⅔ cups basic vegetable stock

¾ cup milk

1 tbsp snipped fresh chives

scant ½ cup heavy cream

salt and pepper

croutons, to garnish (see page 65)

extra virgin olive oil, for drizzling

Goulash Soup

① Heat the oil in a large pan. Add the onion, garlic, and carrots and cook over low heat, stirring occasionally, for 8–10 minutes, until lightly colored. Add the cabbage and bell pepper and cook, stirring frequently, for 3–4 minutes.

② Sprinkle in the flour and paprika and cook, stirring constantly, for 1 minute. Gradually stir in the basic vegetable stock, a little at a time. Increase the heat to medium and bring to a boil, stirring constantly. Season with salt, reduce the heat, cover, and simmer for 30 minutes.

③ Add the potatoes and bring back to a boil, then reduce the heat, re-cover the pan, and simmer for another 20–30 minutes, until the potatoes are soft but not falling apart.

④ Taste and adjust the seasoning and add the sugar, if necessary. Ladle the soup into warmed bowls, swirl a little crème fraîche on top of each, and serve immediately.

Serves 6

2 tbsp olive oil

1 large onion, chopped

2 garlic cloves, finely chopped

3–4 carrots, thinly sliced

½ savoy cabbage, cored and shredded

1 small red bell pepper, seeded and chopped

1 tbsp all-purpose flour

2 tbsp sweet paprika

4 cups basic vegetable stock

2 potatoes, cut into chunks

1–2 teaspoons sugar (optional)

salt and pepper

crème fraîche, to garnish

33

Bacon & Pumpkin Soup

1. Heat the oil in a large pan. Add the onions and cook over low heat, stirring occasionally, for 5 minutes, until softened.

2. Add the pumpkin, bacon, and nutmeg, stir well, then cover and simmer, stirring occasionally, for 5–8 minutes.

3. Pour in the basic vegetable stock, increase the heat to medium, and bring to a boil. Reduce the heat and simmer for 10–15 minutes.

4. Meanwhile, make the bacon croutons. Heat the oil in a skillet. Add the bacon and fry for 4–6 minutes on each side, until crisp and all the fat has been released. Meanwhile, cut the bread into ½-inch/1-cm squares. Remove the bacon from the skillet and drain on paper towels. Add the bread squares and cook, turning and tossing until golden brown all over. Remove from the pan and drain on paper towels.

5. Remove the pan from the heat and let cool slightly. Transfer the soup to a food processor or blender, in batches, if necessary, and process until smooth. Return to the rinsed-out pan, season to taste with salt and pepper, and reheat gently, stirring occasionally.

6. Remove the soup from the heat and ladle into warmed bowls. Sprinkle with the croutons, crumble the bacon over the bowls, and serve immediately.

Serves 6

2 tbsp olive oil

2 onions, chopped

1 lb 5 oz/600 g canned unsweetened pumpkin

generous 1 cup diced smoked bacon

pinch of grated nutmeg

5 cups basic vegetable stock

salt and pepper

Bacon croutons

2 tbsp sunflower oil

4 slices smoked bacon

2 slices day-old bread, crusts removed

Lentil Soup with Ham

1. Heat the oil in a large pan. Add the onion, garlic, celery, carrot, and potato and cook over low heat, stirring occasionally, for 5–7 minutes, until softened. Add the ham and cook, stirring occasionally, for another 3 minutes. Remove from the pan with a slotted spoon and set aside.

2. Add the lentils, basic vegetable stock, bay leaf, and parsley sprigs to the pan, increase the heat to medium, and bring to a boil. Reduce the heat and simmer, stirring occasionally, for 30 minutes.

3. Add the tomatoes and return the vegetables and ham to the pan. Stir well and simmer for 25–30 minutes more.

4. Remove and discard the bay leaf and parsley. Stir in the paprika and vinegar, season to taste with salt and pepper, and heat through for 2–3 minutes. Ladle into a warmed tureen or individual bowls and serve immediately.

Serves 6

3 tbsp olive oil

1 Bermuda onion, chopped

3 garlic cloves, chopped

2 celery stalks, chopped

1 carrot, chopped

1 potato chopped

1 cup chopped smoked ham

2 cups green or brown lentils

⁕ 13 cups basic vegetable stock

1 bay leaf

4 fresh parsley sprigs

4 tomatoes, peeled and chopped

1½ teaspoons sweet paprika

4 tablespoons sherry vinegar

salt and pepper

Lamb & Vegetable Broth

1. Put the lamb into a large pan, pour in the basic vegetable stock, and bring to a boil over medium–low heat, skimming off the foam that rises to the surface.

2. Add the onion, barley, peas, and thyme sprig and bring back to a boil. Reduce the heat, cover, and simmer for 1 hour.

3. Increase the heat to medium, add the leeks, rutabaga, carrots, and cabbage, season with salt and pepper, and bring back to a boil. Stir, reduce the heat, cover, and simmer for 30 minutes, until the meat and vegetables are tender.

4. Skim off any fat from the surface of the soup and taste and adjust the seasoning, if necessary. Ladle into warmed bowls, sprinkle with parsley, and serve immediately.

Serves 6

2 lb 4 oz/1 kg boneless lamb, cut into cubes

7½ cups basic vegetable stock

1 onion, chopped

¼ cup pearl barley

⅓ cup dried green peas, soaked overnight in water to cover, and drained

1 fresh thyme sprig

2 leeks, chopped

1 rutabaga or turnip, chopped

2 carrots, chopped

½ savoy cabbage, cored and shredded

2 tbsp chopped fresh flat-leaf parsley, to garnish

salt and pepper

36

Lamb & Eggplant Soup

1. Preheat the oven to 400°F/200°C. Prick the eggplants in several places with a fork and put them on a cookie sheet. Bake, turning once or twice, for 50–60 minutes, until soft, then remove from the oven and let cool.

2. Meanwhile, heat the oil in a large pan. Add the lamb and cook over medium heat, turning frequently, for 8–10 minutes, until lightly browned all over. Add the basic vegetable stock and onion and bring to a boil. Reduce the heat and simmer for 1½ hours.

3. Remove the lamb from the pan with a slotted spoon and let cool slightly. Add the potatoes, cinnamon, coriander, and cumin to the pan, stir well, and bring back to a boil. Reduce the heat and simmer for 20–25 minutes, until the potatoes have softened.

4. Meanwhile, cut the meat off the bones and chop into bite-size pieces. Peel the eggplants and coarsely chop the flesh.

5. Remove the pan from the heat and let cool slightly. Remove and discard the cinnamon stick. Ladle the soup into a food processor or blender, in batches if necessary, add the eggplants, and process to a puree.

6. Return the puree to the rinsed-out pan, add the lamb and parsley, season to taste with salt and pepper, and reheat gently, stirring occasionally. Garnish with lemon slices and serve with rye bread.

Serves 6

2 eggplants

2 tbsp olive oil

4 lb/1.8 kg lamb shanks or shoulder of lamb

11¼ cups basic vegetable stock

1 large onion, chopped

2 potatoes, cut into chunks

1 cinnamon stick

½ tsp ground coriander

½ tsp ground cumin

3 tbsp chopped fresh flat-leaf parsley

salt and pepper

lemon slices, halved, to garnish

rye bread, to serve

Lamb & Lemon Soup

1. Put the flour into a plastic bag and season with salt and pepper. Add the cubes of lamb, a few at a time, seal the bag, and shake to coat. Shake off any excess.

2. Heat the oil in a large pan. Add the lamb and cook over medium heat, stirring frequently, for 8–10 minutes, until lightly browned all over. Pour in the basic vegetable stock and bring to a boil, skimming off the foam that rises to the surface.

3. Add the carrots, onions, and cayenne pepper, season with salt and pepper, and bring back to a boil. Reduce the heat, cover, and simmer for 1½–2 hours, until the meat is tender.

4. For the garnish, melt the butter in a pan over very low heat or in a microwave-safe bowl in the microwave. Remove from the heat and stir in the cinnamon and paprika.

5. Beat the egg yolks with the lemon juice in a bowl. Remove the pan from the heat and whisk a ladleful of the hot soup into the egg mixture, then add it to the pan. Return the pan to very low heat and heat through, gently rotating the pan, for 1–2 minutes; do not let the soup boil.

6. Ladle the soup into a warm tureen, spoon the spiced melted butter over the top, sprinkle with the mint, and serve immediately, accompanied by flatbreads.

Serves 6

½ cup all-purpose flour

1 lb 2 oz/500 g boneless leg of lamb, cut into cubes

3 tbsp olive oil

5 cups basic vegetable stock

2 carrots, cut into chunks

2 onions, cut into quarters

1 tsp cayenne pepper

3 egg yolks

2 tbsp lemon juice

salt and pepper

flatbreads, to serve

To garnish
4 tablespoons butter

½ tsp ground cinnamon

2 tsp sweet or hot paprika

3 tbsp chopped fresh mint

38

Cream of Chicken Soup

1. Put the chicken into a large pan, pour in the basic vegetable stock, add the bouquet garni, and season with salt and pepper. Bring to a boil over medium heat, skimming off the foam that rises to the surface. Reduce the heat, cover, and simmer for 1–1¼ hours, until the chicken is tender.

2. Remove the chicken from the pan and let cool. Strain the stock into a bowl and let cool, then either chill in the refrigerator overnight or in the freezer for 30 minutes.

3. Meanwhile, mash the butter into the flour in a small bowl to make a paste.

4. Remove and discard the chicken skin, cut the meat off the bones, and chop coarsely. Remove any fat that has solidified on the surface of the stock. Put the chicken and stock into a food processor, in batches if necessary, and process to a smooth puree.

5. Transfer the puree to the rinsed-out pan and heat gently. Gradually whisk in the butter-and-flour mixture, in small pieces at a time, making sure each piece has been fully incorporated before adding the next. Bring to a boil, stirring constantly, then reduce the heat, and simmer for 5 minutes. Taste and adjust the seasoning, if necessary, and stir in the cream. Serve immediately, garnished with croutons.

Serves 6

1 chicken, about 3 lb/1.3 kg

6¾ cups basic vegetable stock

1 bouquet garni (3 fresh parsley sprigs, 2 fresh thyme sprigs, 1 fresh tarragon sprig, and 1 bay leaf, tied together)

1 tbsp butter, softened

2 tbsp all-purpose flour

4 tbsp heavy cream

salt and pepper

croutons, to garnish (see page 65)

39

Cream of Clam Soup

1. Melt the butter in a pan. Add the onion and garlic and cook over low heat, stirring occasionally, for 5 minutes, until softened.

2. Stir in the flour and cook, stirring constantly, for 1 minute, then remove the pan from the heat. Gradually stir in the basic vegetable stock, a little at a time, then stir in the wine.

3. Return the pan to medium heat, add the bay leaf and parsley sprigs, season with salt and pepper, and bring to a boil, stirring constantly. Reduce the heat, cover, and simmer for 15 minutes.

4. Meanwhile, drain the clams, reserving the juices. Finely chop the clams.

5. Add the clams and the reserved juices to the pan, bring back to a boil, and simmer for 5 minutes more.

6. Remove and discard the bay leaf and parsley sprigs. Gradually stir in the cream and heat through gently; do not let the soup boil. Taste and adjust the seasoning, if necessary, and ladle into warmed bowls. Sprinkle with the chopped parsley and serve immediately with whole wheat bread.

Serves 6

3 tbsp butter

1 large onion, finely chopped

2 garlic cloves, finely chopped

1 tbsp all-purpose flour

1¾ cups basic vegetable stock

½ cup medium-dry white wine

1 bay leaf

6 fresh parsley sprigs

1 lb 7 oz/650 g bottled or canned clams

generous 1 cup light cream

salt and pepper

3 tbsp chopped fresh flat-leaf parsley, to garnish

whole wheat bread, to serve

Cajun Crab & Corn Chowder

1. Melt the butter in a large pan. Add the onion, garlic, celery, and carrot and cook over low heat, stirring occasionally, for 5 minutes, until softened.

2. Increase the heat to medium, pour in the wine, and cook for 2 minutes, until the alcohol has evaporated. Pour in the basic vegetable stock and bring to a boil, then add the corn, cayenne, and mixed herbs. Bring back to a boil, reduce the heat, and simmer for 15 minutes.

3. Add the cream and simmer gently over very low heat for 10–15 minutes more; do not let the soup boil.

4. Gradually add the crème fraîche, whisking constantly with a balloon whisk, then stir in the dill and crabmeat, and season to taste with salt and pepper. Heat gently for 3–4 minutes, then serve with whole wheat rolls.

Serves 6

3 tbsp butter
1 onion, finely chopped
2 garlic cloves, finely chopped
2 celery stalks finely chopped
1 small carrot, finely chopped
¾ cup medium-dry white wine
2¼ cups basic vegetable stock
1½ cups frozen corn kernels
pinch of cayenne pepper
½ tsp dried mixed herbs
1½ cups heavy cream
¾ cup crème fraîche
1 tbsp chopped fresh dill
8 oz/225 g white crabmeat
salt and pepper
whole wheat rolls, to serve

Fish & Corn Soup

1. Put the fish fillets into a heatproof dish that will fit into a steamer and sprinkle with the wine. Put the slices of ginger in a garlic crusher and squeeze out the juice over the fish. You may have to do this in batches. Let marinate for 15 minutes.

2. Pour the basic vegetable stock into a pan and bring to a boil. Put the dish of fish into the steamer and set it over the pan. Cover and steam for 8–10 minutes, until the flesh flakes easily. Remove the steamer and set the dish of fish aside.

3. Add the corn to the stock and bring back to a boil, then stir in the sesame oil and season with salt. Reduce the heat and simmer for 10 minutes.

4. Meanwhile, mash the fish fillets with a fork. Mix the cornstarch to a paste with the water.

5. Add the cornstarch paste to the soup and cook, stirring constantly, until thickened. Add the fish and cook for 2–3 minutes, or until heated through.

6. Taste and adjust the seasoning, if necessary, then ladle into warmed bowls. Sprinkle with the scallions and serve immediately.

Serves 6

1 lb 7 oz/650 g sea bass or porgy fillets, skinned

2 tsp Chinese rice wine or dry sherry

¾-inch/2-cm piece of fresh ginger, thinly sliced

5⅔ cups basic vegetable stock

2 cups frozen corn kernels

1 tsp sesame oil

2½ tsp cornstarch

3 tbsp water

2 scallions, chopped

salt

42

Carrot & Mussel Soup

1. Reserve 3 carrots and slice the remainder. Melt 4 tablespoons of the butter in a large pan. Add the sliced carrots and half the sugar and cook over low heat, stirring occasionally, for 5 minutes. Increase the heat to medium, pour in the basic vegetable stock, season with salt, and bring to a boil. Reduce the heat, cover, and simmer, stirring occasionally, for 25 minutes.

2. Meanwhile, finely chop the reserved carrots. Melt the remaining butter in a small pan. Add the carrots and the remaining sugar and cook over low heat, stirring occasionally, for 10 minutes, then remove from the heat.

3. Scrub the mussels under cold running water and pull off the "beards." Discard any with broken shells or that do not shut immediately when sharply tapped. Put them into a pan, pour in the wine, and add the garlic. Cover and cook over high heat, shaking the pan occasionally, for 4–5 minutes, until they open. Remove the pan from the heat and lift out the mussels. Discard any that remain shut. Remove the mussels from the half shell. Strain the cooking liquid through a cheesecloth-lined strainer into a bowl. Remove the pan of carrots from the heat and let cool slightly, then ladle into a food processor, add the mussels cooking liquid, and process. Return the soup to the rinsed-out pan, season to taste, and reheat gently for 3–4 minutes. Ladle into a warmed tureen, gently stir in the mussels, sprinkle with the parsley, and serve with whole wheat rolls.

Serves 6

2 lb 4 oz/1 kg carrots

7 tbsp butter

1 tsp sugar

5⅔ cups basic vegetable stock

48 mussels

1¼ cups dry white wine

1 garlic clove, coarsely chopped

salt and pepper

2 tbsp chopped fresh flat-leaf parsley, to garnish

whole wheat rolls, to serve

Stylish

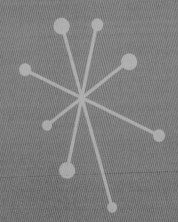

43

Asparagus Soup with Caviar

1. Trim off and reserve the woody ends of the asparagus, leaving the spears 2¾–3½ inches/7–8 cm long. Pour the basic vegetable stock into a pan, add the woody asparagus ends, and bring to a boil. Reduce the heat and simmer for 15 minutes. Meanwhile, cut the remaining asparagus into 1-inch/2.5 cm lengths.

2. Bring a pan of lightly salted water to a boil. Add half the asparagus tips and simmer for 7–10 minutes, until tender. Remove from the heat, drain, and reserve. Remove the basic vegetable stock from the heat and strain into a bowl. Discard the woody asparagus ends.

3. Melt 3 tablespoons of the butter in a large pan, add the leeks and remaining asparagus, and cook over low heat, stirring occasionally, for 5 minutes. Pour in the stock, season with salt and pepper, and bring to a boil over medium heat. Reduce the heat, cover, and simmer for 10–15 minutes, until the asparagus is tender. Remove the pan from the heat and let cool slightly. Ladle the soup into a food processor or blender, in batches if necessary, and process to a smooth puree.

4. Melt the remaining butter in a pan. Stir in the flour and cook, stirring constantly, for 1 minute. Stir in the puree and bring to a boil, stirring constantly. Add the milk and cook, stirring, for a few minutes more, then stir in the cream and reserved asparagus tips. Ladle the soup into warmed bowls, top each with a teaspoonful of caviar, and serve immediately.

Serves 6

1 lb 2 oz/500 g asparagus spears
4 cups basic vegetable stock
5 tbsp butter
1½ cups thinly sliced leeks
¼ cup all-purpose flour
⅔ cup milk
6 tbsp heavy cream
salt and pepper
6 tsp caviar or keta (salmon roe), to garnish

44

Avocado Soup

1. Halve the avocados lengthwise and gently twist the halves apart. Remove and discard the pits and scoop out the flesh. Chop into small pieces, put them into a bowl, sprinkle with the lemon juice, and toss well to coat. Melt the butter in a pan. Add the shallots and cook over low heat, stirring occasionally, for 5 minutes, until softened. Stir in the flour and cook, stirring constantly, for 1 minute.

2. Remove the pan from the heat and gradually stir in the basic vegetable stock. Return the pan to medium heat and bring to a boil, stirring constantly. Add the avocados, reduce the heat, cover, and simmer for 15 minutes.

3. Meanwhile, preheat the broiler. Make the guacamole croutes. Toast the bread on one side under the broiler. Turn the slices over, brush with the oil, and toast. Remove from the heat. Scoop out the avocado flesh into a bowl and mash with the lime juice and chili sauce, to taste, and season. Divide the avocado mixture among the croutes and set aside.

4. Remove the soup from the heat and push it through a strainer set over a bowl, pressing the vegetables with the back of the ladle. Return the soup to the rinsed-out pan, stir in the cream, season to taste, and reheat gently; do not let the soup boil.

5. Ladle the soup into warmed bowls, float the lime slices on top, add the oil, and serve immediately, passing around the guacamole croutes separately.

Serves 6

3 ripe avocados
2 tbsp lemon juice
6 tbsp butter
6 shallots, chopped
1½ tbsp all-purpose flour
3¾ cups basic vegetable stock
¾ cup light cream
1 lime, thinly sliced
salt and pepper
extra virgin olive oil,
    for drizzling

Guacamole croutes
6 thin slices of day-old
    baguette
olive oil, for brushing
½ large ripe avocado, pitted
    and brushed with lime juice
juice of 1 lime
¼–¾ tsp chili or Tabasco sauce
salt and pepper

Broccoli & Roquefort Soup

1. Melt the butter in a large pan. Add the onions and potato and stir well. Cover and cook over low heat for 7 minutes. Add the broccoli and stir well, then re-cover the pan, and cook for 5 minutes more.

2. Increase the heat to medium, pour in the basic vegetable stock, and bring to a boil. Reduce the heat, season with salt and pepper, re-cover, and simmer for 15–20 minutes, until the vegetables are tender.

3. Remove the pan from the heat, strain into a bowl, reserving the vegetables, and let cool slightly. Put the vegetables into a food processor, add 1 ladleful of the stock, and process to a smooth puree. With the motor running, gradually add the remaining stock.

4. Return the soup to the rinsed-out pan and reheat gently until very hot but not boiling. Remove from the heat and stir in the cheese until melted and thoroughly combined. Stir in the mace and taste and adjust the seasoning, if necessary. Ladle into warmed bowls, sprinkle with the croutons, and serve immediately.

Serves 6

3 tbsp butter

2 white onions, chopped

1 large potato, chopped

1 lb 10 oz/750 g broccoli, cut into small florets

6¾ cups basic vegetable stock

5½ oz/150 g Roquefort cheese, diced

pinch of ground mace

salt and pepper

croutons, to garnish (see page 65)

Spicy Cucumber Soup

1. Pour the basic vegetable stock into a pan, add the lemongrass, 2 tablespoons of the lime juice, and the cilantro sprigs and bring to a boil over medium heat. Reduce the heat, cover, and simmer for 25 minutes.

2. Remove the pan from the heat and strain the stock into a clean pan. Stir in the remaining lime juice and the cucumber and season to taste with salt and pepper.

3. Bring back to a boil, stirring constantly, then reduce the heat, and simmer for 5 minutes.

4. Remove the pan from the heat, taste, and adjust the seasoning, if necessary, and ladle into individual bowls. Divide the scallions, chiles, and cilantro among the bowls and serve immediately.

Serves 6

5 cups basic vegetable stock

2 tbsp chopped lemongrass

3½ tbsp lime juice

16 fresh cilantro sprigs

6 oz/175 g cucumber, peeled and cut into julienne strips

salt and pepper

To garnish
3 scallions, thinly sliced

3 green chiles, seeded and finely chopped

2 tbsp chopped fresh cilantro

47

Vegetable Broth

1. Pour the basic vegetable stock into a pan and bring to a boil over medium heat. Add the corn cobs and carrots and cook for 3 minutes, then add the snow peas, mushrooms, and Chinese cabbage, and cook for another 2 minutes.

2. Add the Chinese chives and soy sauce and season to taste with salt, if necessary (soy sauce is very salty), and pepper. Simmer for 2–3 minutes more, then ladle into warmed bowls, garnish with the scallions, and serve immediately.

Serves 6

* 4 cups basic vegetable stock

¾ cup baby corn cobs, thinly sliced diagonally

⅓ cup baby carrots, thinly sliced diagonally

1 cup snow peas or green beans, sliced diagonally

1¼ cups thinly sliced cremini mushrooms

3 oz/85 g Chinese cabbage or spinach, shredded

1 tbsp chopped Chinese chives

2 tbsp light soy sauce

salt and pepper

thinly sliced scallions, to garnish

Vegetable Soup with Semolina Dumplings

1. First, make the dumplings. Pour the milk into a pan and add the water, sugar, nutmeg, and a pinch of salt. Bring to a boil over medium heat, then reduce the heat, and sprinkle the semolina over the surface of the liquid. Simmer, stirring constantly, until thickened, then remove the pan from the heat and let cool for 15 minutes. Stir in the beaten egg until thoroughly combined, then cover, and chill in the refrigerator for 30 minutes.

2. To make the soup, blanch the turnips and carrots in a pan of boiling water for 3 minutes, then drain. Melt the butter in a large pan, add the turnips and carrots, and cook over low heat, stirring frequently, for 5 minutes.

3. Sprinkle the sugar over the vegetables, increase the heat to medium, and cook, stirring constantly, until they begin to caramelize. Pour in the basic vegetable stock, season with salt and pepper, and bring to a boil, then reduce the heat, and simmer for 20 minutes.

4. Meanwhile, flour your hands and shape the semolina mixture into small balls. About 7–10 minutes before the end of the cooking time, add the dumplings to the soup and simmer until they have risen to the surface.

5. Taste and adjust the seasoning, if necessary, and ladle the soup into warmed bowls. Sprinkle with the parsley and serve immediately.

Serves 6

⅓ cup diced turnip

scant 1 cup diced carrots

4 tbsp butter

1½ tsp sugar

7½ cups basic vegetable stock

salt and pepper

3 tbsp chopped fresh flat-leaf parsley, to garnish

Dumplings
5 tbsp milk

⅔ cup water

1 tsp sugar

pinch of grated nutmeg

¾ cup semolina

1 extra large egg, lightly beaten

all-purpose flour, for dusting

salt

Curried Vegetable Soup

1. Melt the butter in a large pan. Add the onions and garlic and cook over low heat, stirring occasionally, for 8–10 minutes, until lightly browned. Stir in the cumin and coriander and cook, stirring constantly, for 2 minutes. Add the sweet potato, carrots, and parsnips and cook, stirring frequently, for 5 minutes, then stir in the curry paste, and mix well. Increase the heat to medium, pour in the basic vegetable stock, and bring to a boil, stirring occasionally. Reduce the heat, cover, and simmer for 20–25 minutes, until the vegetables are tender.

2. Meanwhile, make the garnish. Cut the ginger in half and then into thin julienne strips. Heat the oil in a small skillet over high heat. Reduce the heat, add the ginger, and cook, stirring and twisting constantly, for 1 minute. Remove with a slotted spoon and drain on paper towels.

3. Remove the pan of soup from the heat and let cool slightly. Ladle the soup into a food processor or blender, in batches if necessary, and process to a puree.

4. Return the soup to the rinsed-out pan and stir in the milk. Cook, stirring occasionally, for 5 minutes. Stir in the lime juice and 3 tablespoons of the sour cream and season to taste with salt and pepper.

5. Ladle the soup into warmed bowls, add a swirl of the remaining sour cream, and garnish with the fried ginger. Serve immediately with naan.

Serves 6

3 tbsp butter
2 onions, chopped
2 garlic cloves, finely chopped
1½ tsp ground cumin
1 tsp ground coriander
1 sweet potato, chopped
2 carrots, chopped
3 parsnips chopped
1 tbsp curry paste
3 cups basic vegetable stock
3 cups milk
1 tsp lime juice
6 tbsp sour cream
salt and pepper
naan, to serve

To garnish
4-inch/10-cm piece fresh
   ginger
2 tbsp peanut oil

50

Mexican Tomato & Vermicelli Soup

1. Put the onion, garlic, chiles, and tomatoes into a food processor and process to a smooth puree.

2. Heat the oil in a heavy skillet. Add the vermicelli and stir-fry over low heat for a few minutes, until golden brown. Remove from the skillet and drain on paper towels.

3. Add the vegetable puree to the skillet and cook, stirring constantly, for 6–8 minutes, until thickened. Remove the skillet from the heat.

4. Spoon the vegetable puree into a large pan, pour in the basic vegetable stock, stir in the ketchup and tomato paste, and add the vermicelli and cilantro. Season to taste with salt and pepper and bring to a boil. Reduce the heat, cover, and simmer for 5 minutes, or until the vermicelli is tender.

5. Ladle the soup into warmed bowls, sprinkle with the shreds of lime rind, and serve immediately.

Serves 6

1 Bermuda onion, chopped

2 garlic cloves, chopped

1–2 red Serrano chiles, seeded and chopped

2½ cups peeled, seeded, and chopped tomatoes

3 tbsp corn oil

3 oz/85 g vermicelli

6¾ cups basic vegetable stock

1 tbsp ketchup

1 tbsp tomato paste

1 tbsp chopped fresh cilantro

salt and pepper

finely shredded lime rind, to garnish

Shiitake Mushroom Soup with Egg

1. Pour the basic vegetable stock into a pan, add the kombu, and bring just to a boil over low heat. Immediately remove the kombu. Add the bonito flakes and bring to a boil, then remove the pan from the heat and let the bonito flakes settle. Strain the stock through a cheesecloth-lined strainer into a clean pan.

2. Meanwhile, cut off and discard the mushroom stems and thinly slice the caps.

3. Bring the basic vegetable stock to a boil. Reduce the heat, add the mushrooms, and simmer for 2–3 minutes, until just tender but still firm to the bite. Stir in the Japanese soy sauce and sake and season to taste with salt.

4. Increase the heat to medium–low. Gradually pour in the eggs, moving the bowl continuously around the pan so that they are evenly distributed and set immediately. Simmer for about 15 seconds, then remove the pan from the heat.

5. Break up the "omelet" and divide it and the soup among individual bowls. Garnish with the scallions and serve immediately.

Serves 6

- 3¾ cups basic vegetable stock
- ¼ oz/10 g kombu seaweed
- ½ oz/10 g bonito flakes
- 6 shiitake mushrooms
- 1 tbsp Japanese soy sauce
- 2 tsp sake or dry white wine
- 2 extra large eggs, lightly beaten
- salt
- scallions, thinly sliced, to garnish

Egg Flower Soup

1. Pour the basic vegetable stock into a pan and stir in the rice wine, soy sauce, and sesame oil. Put the slices of ginger into a garlic crusher and squeeze out the juice into the pan. Add the Chinese cabbage leaves and bring to a boil, then reduce the heat, and simmer for 3–4 minutes.

2. Increase the heat to medium–low. Gradually pour the eggs into the center of the soup in a steady stream. Simmer for 2 seconds, then stir to break the eggs into filaments. Season to taste, ladle into warmed bowls, and serve.

Serves 6

4 cups basic vegetable stock

3 tbsp Chinese rice wine or dry sherry

3 tbsp light soy sauce

1 tsp sesame oil

½-inch/1-cm piece fresh ginger, thinly sliced

6 Chinese cabbage leaves or bok choy, shredded

2 eggs, beaten

salt and pepper

53

Garlic Soup

1. Crush the garlic cloves with the flat side of a heavy knife blade, then peel off and discard the skins. Put the garlic cloves into a pan and add the bay leaf, cloves, peppercorns, saffron, parsley sprigs, chervil sprigs, thyme sprigs, sage leaves, and olive oil.

2. Pour in the basic vegetable stock and bring to a boil, then reduce the heat, cover, and simmer for 40 minutes.

3. Remove the pan from the heat and strain the soup into a warmed tureen. Season to taste with salt and pepper, sprinkle with the parsley, and serve with whole wheat rolls, passing around the Parmesan separately.

Serves 6

2 garlic bulbs, separated into cloves

1 bay leaf

3 cloves

3 black peppercorns

½ tsp saffron threads

2 fresh flat-leaf parsley sprigs

2 fresh chervil sprigs

4 fresh thyme sprigs

16 fresh sage leaves

1½ tbsp olive oil

7½ cups basic vegetable stock

2 tbsp chopped fresh flat-leaf parsley, to garnish

salt and pepper

To serve
whole wheat rolls
thinly shaved Parmesan cheese

54

Hot & Sour Soup

1. Pour the basic vegetable stock into a pan and add the lime leaves, lemongrass, half the chiles, half the scallions, and the garlic. Bring to a boil, then reduce the heat and simmer for 30 minutes.

2. Remove the pan from the heat and strain the soup into a clean pan. Discard the contents of the strainer.

3. Return the soup to the heat, stir in the lime juice, sugar, cilantro, and remaining chiles and scallions, and season to taste with salt. Bring back to a boil, then reduce the heat, and simmer for 5 minutes. Add the tofu and carrots and simmer for another 4–5 minutes. Serve immediately.

Serves 6

5⅔ cups basic vegetable stock

6 fresh or dried kaffir lime leaves

3 lemongrass stalks, cut into 1½-inch/4-cm lengths

3 fresh red chiles, seeded and sliced

6 scallions, thinly sliced

3 garlic cloves, thinly sliced

6 tbsp lime juice

2 tsp sugar

2 tbsp chopped fresh cilantro

12 oz/350 g firm tofu, thinly sliced

2 carrots, thinly sliced

salt

55

Pork Rib Soup with Pickled Mustard Greens

1. Heat the oil in a small skillet or wok. Add the garlic and stir-fry for a few minutes, until golden. Transfer to a plate and set aside.

2. Pour the basic vegetable stock into a pan and bring to a boil over medium heat. Add the spareribs and bring back to a boil, then reduce the heat, cover, and simmer for 15 minutes, until tender.

3. Meanwhile, put the cellophane noodles into a bowl, pour in hot water to cover, and let soak for 10 minutes, until softened. Drain well.

4. Add the noodles and pickled greens to the soup and bring back to a boil. Stir in the Thai fish sauce and sugar, season to taste with pepper, and ladle into warmed bowls. Garnish with the garlic slices and red and green chiles and serve immediately.

Serves 6

1 tbsp peanut oil

3 garlic cloves, thinly sliced

5 cups basic vegetable stock

1 lb 2 oz/500 g pork finger spareribs

3 oz/85 g cellophane noodles

10 oz/280 g canned Thai pickled mustard greens or Chinese snow pickles, well-rinsed and coarsely chopped

2 tbsp Thai fish sauce

½ tsp sugar

pepper

1 red and 1 green chile, seeded and thinly sliced, to garnish

56

Chicken Noodle Soup

1. Bring a pan of water to a boil. Add the noodles and cook according to the instructions on the package. Drain, refresh under cold running water, and let stand in a bowl of water.

2. Heat the oil in a large pan. Add the scallions and bacon and cook over low heat, stirring occasionally, for 5 minutes, until the scallions have softened and the bacon is beginning to color.

3. Add the tarragon and chicken, increase the heat to medium, and cook, stirring frequently, for about 8 minutes, until the chicken is golden brown all over.

4. Pour in the wine and cook for 2 minutes, until the alcohol has evaporated, then pour enough of the basic vegetable stock just to cover the meat. Reduce the heat, cover, and simmer for 20–30 minutes, until the chicken is tender.

5. Pour in the remaining stock, season with salt and pepper, and bring to a boil. Add the noodles and heat through briefly. Ladle the soup into warmed bowls and serve immediately with crusty bread, passing around the Parmesan separately.

Serves 6

6 oz/175 g egg noodles
2 tbsp olive oil
1 cup chopped scallions
4 bacon slices, chopped
2 tsp chopped fresh tarragon
6 skinless boneless chicken thighs, diced
⅔ cup dry white wine
5 cups basic vegetable stock
salt and pepper

To serve
grated Parmesan cheese
crusty bread

Crab & Noodle Soup

1. Bring a pan of water to a boil. Add the noodles and cook according to the instructions on the package. Drain, refresh under cold running water, and let stand in a bowl of water.

2. Heat the oil in a large pan. Add the shallots, carrots, and celery and cook over low heat, stirring occasionally, for 5 minutes, until softened.

3. Increase the heat to medium, pour in the vermouth, and cook for 2 minutes, until the alcohol has evaporated. Pour in the basic vegetable stock and bring to a boil, then reduce the heat and simmer for 10 minutes.

4. Meanwhile, flake the crabmeat and remove any pieces of shell or cartilage. Drain the noodles and add them to the pan. Add the crab and stir in the anchovy essence and lemon juice. Season to taste with salt and pepper. Simmer for a few minutes more to heat through, then ladle the soup into warmed bowls, garnish with the chopped parsley, and serve immediately.

Serves 6

5 oz/150 g egg noodles

3 tbsp peanut oil

4 shallots, chopped

2 carrots, chopped

2 celery stalks, chopped

6 tbsp dry vermouth

7½ cups basic vegetable stock

6 oz/175 g white crabmeat, thawed if frozen

a few drops of anchovy essence

1 tbsp lemon juice

salt and pepper

chopped fresh flat-leaf parsley, to garnish

Shrimp Bisque

① Melt the butter in a large pan. Add the onion, carrots, celery, and bay leaves and cook over low heat, stirring occasionally, for 8–10 minutes, until golden brown. Increase the heat to medium, add the shrimp, and cook, stirring occasionally, for 4–5 minutes, until they change color.

② Pour in the brandy and wine and cook for 4–5 minutes more, until the alcohol has evaporated and the shrimp are cooked. Remove the shrimp with a slotted spoon and let cool slightly.

③ Add the tomatoes, tomato paste, parsley, and basic vegetable stock to the pan and bring to a boil. Meanwhile, peel the shrimp, reserving the shells. Add the shells to the pan, reduce the heat, and simmer for 30 minutes. Devein the shrimp by cutting a slit along their backs with a sharp knife and removing the black vein with the point of the knife. Chop the shrimp.

④ Remove the soup from the heat, add the chopped shrimp, and let cool slightly. Ladle the soup into a food processor, in batches if necessary, and process. Pour the soup through a strainer into the rinsed-out pan, pressing the contents of the strainer with the back of a ladle to extract the liquid. Bring the soup back to a boil, then reduce the heat, and stir in the cream, lemon juice, and cayenne. Taste and adjust the seasoning, if necessary, and heat for 1–2 minutes more; do not let the soup boil. Ladle into warmed bowls, decorate with the heavy cream, and add some cayenne. Serve with crusty bread.

Serves 6

6 tbsp butter

1 small onion, chopped

2 small carrots, chopped

1 celery stalk, chopped

2 bay leaves

1 lb 7 oz/650 g unpeeled shrimp

3 tbsp brandy

scant ½ cup dry white wine

1 lb 7 oz/650 g tomatoes, chopped

1½ tsp tomato paste

2 fresh parsley sprigs

11¼ cups basic vegetable stock

6 tbsp heavy cream, plus extra to decorate

1 tbsp lemon juice

pinch of cayenne pepper or dash of Tabasco sauce, plus extra to decorate

salt and pepper

crusty bread, to serve

Cool

59

Al Fresco Avocado Soup

1. Halve the avocados lengthwise and gently twist the halves apart. Remove and discard the pits and, using a teaspoon, scoop out the flesh.

2. Put the avocado flesh, lemon juice, basic vegetable stock, shallot, and chili and garlic sauce into a food processor or blender and process to a smooth puree. Scrape into a bowl and whisk in the cream with a balloon whisk. Season to taste with salt and pepper.

3. Cover tightly with plastic wrap and chill in the refrigerator for at least 3 hours. To serve, stir the soup and taste and adjust the seasoning, if necessary. Ladle into individual bowls, garnish with watercress sprigs, and serve immediately.

Serves 6

2 avocados

1 tbsp lemon juice

✳ 4 cups basic vegetable stock

1 shallot, chopped

dash of chili and garlic sauce

⅔ cup heavy cream

salt and pepper

watercress sprigs, to garnish

60

Fava Bean Soup

1. Pour the basic vegetable stock into a pan and bring to a boil. Reduce the heat to a simmer, add the beans, and cook for about 7 minutes, until just tender.

2. Remove the pan from the heat and let cool slightly. Ladle into a food processor or blender, in batches if necessary, and process to a puree. Strain the puree into a bowl to remove the skins.

3. Stir in the lemon juice and summer savory and season to taste with salt and pepper. Let cool completely, then cover with plastic wrap and chill in the refrigerator for at least 3 hours.

4. To serve, stir the soup and taste and adjust the seasoning, if necessary. Ladle into bowls and garnish with the yogurt and fresh mint leaves.

Serves 6

3¾ cups basic vegetable stock

4⅔ cups shelled young fava beans

3 tbsp lemon juice

2 tbsp chopped fresh summer savory

6 tbsp strained plain yogurt, chilled

salt and pepper

fresh mint leaves or marjoram flowers, to garnish

Cucumber & Mint Soup

1. Pour the basic vegetable stock into a large pan, add the scallions, and bring to a boil. Reduce the heat and simmer for 10 minutes. Reserve a little of the diced cucumber for the garnish and add the remainder and the mint sprigs to the pan. Simmer for another 20 minutes. Remove the pan from the heat and let cool slightly.

2. Remove and discard the mint sprigs. Ladle the soup into a food processor or blender, in batches if necessary, and process to a puree. Return the soup to the rinsed-out pan and reheat gently.

3. Mix the cornstarch to a paste with the water in a bowl. Stir the paste into the pan and bring to a boil, stirring constantly. Simmer, stirring constantly, for a few minutes, until thickened.

4. Stir in the cream and season to taste with salt and pepper. Remove the pan from the heat and stir in a few drops of food coloring, if using, to give the soup an attractive pale green color.

5. Ladle into bowls, garnish with the reserved cucumber and fresh mint leaves, and drizzle over the oil. Serve with warm pita bread.

Serves 6

5⅔ cups basic vegetable stock

6 scallions, chopped

2 cucumbers, peeled, seeded, and diced

3 fresh mint sprigs

1½ tbsp cornstarch

3 tbsp water

5 tbsp heavy cream

green food coloring (optional)

salt and pepper

fresh mint leaves, to garnish

extra virgin olive oil, for drizzling

warm pita bread, to serve

Curried Cucumber Soup

1. Whisk together the crème fraîche, 1 cup of the yogurt, the curry powder, and cayenne pepper in a bowl until thoroughly combined.

2. Stir in the onion, cucumbers, cilantro, and basic vegetable stock and season to taste with salt and pepper. Cover with plastic wrap and chill in the refrigerator for at least 3 hours. Chill the remaining yogurt.

3. To serve, stir the soup and taste and adjust the seasoning, if necessary. Ladle into bowls, garnish with the remaining yogurt and fresh cilantro sprigs, and serve with garlic naan.

Serves 6

½ cup crème fraîche

1½ cups plain yogurt

1–1½ tsp curry powder

pinch of cayenne pepper

1 white onion, grated

2 cucumbers, peeled, seeded, and diced

4 tbsp finely chopped fresh cilantro

1¼ cups basic vegetable stock

salt and pepper

fresh cilantro sprigs, to garnish

garlic naan, to serve

63

Pea Soup

1. Pour the basic vegetable stock into a pan, add the onion and garlic, and bring to a boil over medium heat. Reduce the heat and simmer for 15 minutes.

2. Increase the heat to medium, add the peas, mint, lavender, if using, and sugar, and bring back to a boil. Reduce the heat and simmer for another 5–7 minutes.

3. Remove the pan from the heat and let cool completely. Remove and discard the herb sprigs. Ladle the soup into a food processor or blender, in batches if necessary, and process to a smooth puree.

4. Transfer to a bowl and stir in the lemon juice and sour cream. Season to taste with salt and pepper, cover with plastic wrap, and chill in the refrigerator for at least 3 hours. To serve, stir well, taste and adjust the seasoning, if necessary, and ladle into bowls.

Serves 6

3¾ cups basic vegetable stock

1 Bermuda onion, finely chopped

2 garlic cloves, finely chopped

3 cups frozen baby peas

2 fresh mint sprigs

1 fresh lavender sprig (optional)

½ tsp sugar

1 tbsp lemon juice

1 cup sour cream or plain yogurt

salt and pepper

Asparagus Soup

1. Cut off the tips of the asparagus and set aside. Cut the remaining spears into ½-inch/1-cm lengths.

2. Melt the butter in a large pan. Add the scallions and cook over low heat, stirring occasionally, for 5 minutes. Add the pieces of asparagus spears and cook, stirring occasionally, for another 5 minutes.

3. Stir in the flour and cook, stirring constantly, for 2 minutes. Remove the pan from the heat and gradually stir in the basic vegetable stock. Return the pan to medium heat and bring to a boil, stirring constantly. Reduce the heat, season with salt and pepper, and simmer for 35–40 minutes.

4. Meanwhile, bring a pan of water to a boil. Add the asparagus tips and cook for 5–8 minutes, until tender. Drain and cut in half.

5. Remove the soup from the heat and let cool slightly. Ladle it into a food processor or blender, in batches if necessary, and process to a smooth puree. Pour the soup into a bowl and stir in the crème fraîche, lemon rind, and asparagus tips. Let cool completely, then cover with plastic wrap, and chill in the refrigerator for at least 3 hours.

6. To serve, stir the soup and taste and adjust the seasoning, if necessary. Ladle into bowls, add the Parmesan, and serve with melba toast.

Serves 6

2¼ lb/1 kg asparagus, trimmed
4 tbsp butter
6 scallions, chopped
3 tbsp all-purpose flour
6¼ cups basic vegetable stock
½ cup crème fraîche
1 tsp finely grated lemon rind
salt and pepper

To serve
grated Parmesan cheese
melba toast

Carrot & Orange Soup

1. Melt the butter in a large pan. Add the shallots and carrots and cook over low heat, stirring occasionally, for 5–8 minutes, until softened.

2. Pour in the stock, increase the heat to medium, and bring to a boil. Season with salt and pepper, reduce the heat, cover, and simmer for 1 hour.

3. Remove the pan from the heat and let cool slightly. Ladle the soup into a food processor or blender, in batches if necessary, and process to a smooth puree.

4. Transfer the soup to a bowl and stir in the orange juice and orange rind. Let cool completely, then cover with plastic wrap and chill in the refrigerator for at least 3 hours.

5. To serve, stir in the cream, taste and adjust the seasoning, if necessary, and ladle into bowls.

Serves 6

3 tbsp butter

4 shallots, chopped

1 lb 5 oz/600 g baby carrots, sliced

4 cups basic vegetable stock

1½ cups orange juice

grated rind of 1 orange

⅔ cup light cream, chilled

salt and pepper

66

Beet & Egg Soup

1. Put the beets and lemons into a large pan, pour in the basic vegetable stock, and bring to a boil. Reduce the heat and simmer for 20 minutes.

2. Remove the pan from the heat and let cool slightly. Ladle the soup into a food processor or blender, in batches if necessary, and process to a puree. Pass the soup through a strainer into a bowl to remove any membrane or fibers. Let cool completely.

3. Meanwhile, put the eggs, honey, and a pinch of salt into a food processor blender and process until thoroughly combined. Gradually add the mixture to the soup, stirring constantly.

4. Cover with plastic wrap and chill in the refrigerator for at least 3 hours. To serve, stir the soup and taste and adjust the seasoning, if necessary. Ladle into bowls, garnish with the sour cream and snipped chives, and drizzle over the honey. Serve.

Serves 6

1 lb 7 oz/650 g cooked beets, peeled and chopped

2 lemons, peeled, seeded, and chopped

5⅔ cups basic vegetable stock

3 extra large eggs

1½ tbsp honey, plus extra for drizzling

salt

To garnish
sour cream, chilled

snipped fresh chives

Vichyssoise

1. Melt the butter in a large pan. Add the leeks and onions and stir well. Cover and cook over low heat, stirring occasionally, for 8–10 minutes, until very soft but not colored.

2. Increase the heat to medium, add the potatoes, pour in the basic vegetable stock, and bring to a boil. Reduce the heat, cover, and simmer for 25 minutes. Stir in the cream, season with salt and pepper, and cook for 5 minutes more; do not let the soup boil.

3. Remove the pan from the heat and let cool slightly. Ladle the soup into a food processor or blender, in batches if necessary, and process to a smooth puree.

4. Pour the soup into a bowl and let cool completely. Cover with plastic wrap and chill in the refrigerator for at least 3 hours.

5. To serve, stir the soup and taste and adjust the seasoning, if necessary. Ladle into bowls, garnish with the snipped chives, and serve immediately.

Serves 6

3 tbsp butter

1 lb 4 oz/550 g leeks, finely chopped

1½ onions, chopped

8 oz/225 g potatoes, thickly sliced

5⅔ cups basic vegetable stock

1½ cups heavy cream

salt and pepper

snipped fresh chives, to garnish

Leek, Potato & Pear Soup

1. Measure 3 tablespoons of the basic vegetable stock into a small bowl, stir in the saffron, and set aside.

2. Melt the butter in a large pan. Add the leeks and potatoes and cook over low heat, stirring occasionally, for 5 minutes, until the leeks have softened.

3. Increase the heat to medium, add the pears, pour in the remaining stock and the saffron mixture, and bring to a boil, stirring frequently. Reduce the heat, cover, and simmer for 20–25 minutes, until the vegetables and pears are tender.

4. Remove the pan from the heat and let cool slightly. Ladle the soup into a food processor or blender, in batches if necessary, and process to a smooth puree.

5. Pour the soup into a bowl, season to taste with salt and pepper, and let cool completely. Cover with plastic wrap and chill in the refrigerator for at least 3 hours.

6. To serve, stir the soup and taste and adjust the seasoning, if necessary. Ladle into bowls, top each with a spoonful of crème fraîche and a sprig of watercress, and serve immediately.

Serves 6

5⅔ cups basic vegetable stock

pinch of saffron strands, lightly crushed

3 tbsp butter

3 cups thinly sliced leeks

⅔ cup diced potatoes

3 ripe pears, peeled, cored, and chopped

salt and pepper

To garnish
crème fraîche, chilled

watercress sprigs

69

Apple & Fennel Soup

1. Melt the butter in a large pan. Add the onion and garlic and cook over low heat, stirring occasionally, for 5 minutes, until softened. Add the fennel and potatoes and cook, stirring occasionally, for another 8–10 minutes.

2. Gradually pour in the hard cider, being careful because it will foam, and cook for 2 minutes, until the alcohol has evaporated. Increase the heat to medium, add the star anise, bouquet garni, lemon juice, and basic vegetable stock, and bring to a boil. Season to taste with salt and pepper, reduce the heat, and simmer for 20–25 minutes, until the vegetables are tender.

3. Remove the pan from the heat and let cool slightly. Remove and discard the star anise and bouquet garni. Ladle the soup into a food processor or blender, in batches if necessary, and process to a smooth puree.

4. Transfer the soup to a bowl and let cool completely. Cover with plastic wrap and chill in the refrigerator for at least 3 hours.

5. Chop the reserved fennel fronds. To serve, stir in the crème fraîche and taste and adjust the seasoning, if necessary. Ladle into bowls, garnish each with a lemon slice and fennel fronds, and serve immediately.

Serves 6

2 tbsp butter

1 small onion, chopped

1 small garlic clove, finely chopped

1 large fennel bulb, fronds reserved, diced

2 potatoes, diced

1¼ cups hard cider

1 star anise

1 bouquet garni (3 fresh parsley sprigs, 2 fresh thyme sprigs, and 1 bay leaf, tied together)

2 tbsp lemon juice

1¼ cups basic vegetable stock

1 cup crème fraîche or strained plain yogurt, chilled

6 lemon slices

salt and pepper

Apple Soup

1. Reserve 2 of the apples and peel, core, and dice the remainder. Put the diced apple into a bowl, add the lemon juice, and toss well to prevent discoloration.

2. Melt 3 tablespoons of the butter in a large pan. Add the leeks and stir well, then cover and cook over low heat, stirring occasionally, for 8–10 minutes, until softened. Add the diced apple and cook, stirring occasionally, for another 5 minutes. Add the potatoes and cook, stirring occasionally, for an additional 5 minutes. Increase the heat to medium, pour in the basic vegetable stock, and bring to a boil. Reduce the heat, cover, and simmer for 45–50 minutes, until the leeks and apples are soft.

3. Remove the pan from the heat and let cool slightly. Ladle the soup into a food processor or blender, in batches if necessary, and process to a smooth puree. Transfer to a bowl, stir in the cream and nutmeg, season to taste with salt and pepper, and let cool completely. Cover with plastic wrap and chill for at least 3 hours.

4. To serve, peel, core, and dice the reserved apples. Melt the remaining butter in a skillet. Add the diced apples and cook over low heat, stirring occasionally, for 5 minutes, until lightly colored and softened but not disintegrating. Remove with a slotted spoon and drain on paper towels. Stir the soup and taste and adjust the seasoning, if necessary. Ladle into bowls, garnish with the fried apples, and serve immediately.

Serves 6

2¼ lb/1 kg apples
2 tbsp lemon juice
5 tbsp butter
2 leeks, sliced
2 potatoes, diced
6¼ cups basic vegetable stock
⅔ cup heavy cream
pinch of grated nutmeg
salt and pepper

Roasted Red Bell Pepper Soup with Garlic Croutons

1. Preheat the broiler. Put the bell peppers on a cookie sheet and broil, turning frequently, for 10 minutes, until the skins are charred. Remove with tongs, put them into a plastic bag, tie the top, and let stand until cool enough to handle. Peel off the skins, halve, and seed, then coarsely chop the flesh.

2. Heat the oil in a large pan. Add the onion and garlic and cook over low heat, stirring occasionally, for 5 minutes, until softened. Add the bell peppers and tomatoes, stir well, cover, and cook, stirring occasionally, for 8–10 minutes, until pulpy. Increase the heat to medium, pour in the wine, and cook for 2 minutes, until the alcohol has evaporated. Stir in the sugar, pour in the basic vegetable stock, and bring to a boil. Season, reduce the heat, and simmer for 30 minutes.

3. Remove the pan from the heat and let cool slightly. Ladle the soup into a food processor or blender, and process to a smooth puree. Transfer to a bowl and let cool completely, then cover with plastic wrap, and chill in the refrigerator for at least 3 hours.

4. To make the garlic croutons, heat the oil in a skillet. Add the garlic and stir-fry over low heat for about 2 minutes. Remove and discard the garlic, add the diced bread, and cook, stirring and tossing frequently, until golden brown.

5. To serve, stir the soup and taste and adjust the seasoning, if necessary. Ladle into bowls, sprinkle with the garlic croutons, drizzle with the chili oil, and serve immediately.

Serves 6

3 red bell peppers

3 tbsp olive oil

1 Bermuda onion, chopped

3 garlic cloves, finely chopped

2¼ lb/1 kg ripe tomatoes, peeled, seeded, and coarsely chopped

6 tbsp red wine

1 tsp sugar

✳ 4 cups basic vegetable stock

salt and pepper

chili oil, for drizzling

Garlic croutons

3 tbsp olive oil

2 garlic cloves, chopped

3 slices of day-old bread, crusts removed, cut into ¼-inch/5-mm dice

72

Quick-and-Easy Chickpea Soup with Sesame Paste

1. Heat a heavy skillet. Add the coriander and cumin seeds and cook over low heat, stirring constantly, for a few minutes, until they give off their aroma. Remove from the heat, tip the seeds into a mortar, and pound with a pestle until ground.

2. Pour the basic vegetable stock into a food processor or blender, add the sesame paste, lemon juice, garlic, and roasted spices and process until thoroughly combined. Pour into a bowl, stir in the mint, and season to taste with salt and pepper. Cover with plastic wrap and chill for 1 hour.

3. To serve, stir the soup and taste and adjust the seasoning. Stir in the chickpeas, ladle into bowls, garnish with the chopped cilantro, and drizzle with the oil. Serve immediately with warm pita bread.

Serves 6

½ tsp coriander seeds

1 tsp cumin seeds

2½ cups basic vegetable stock

2 cups sesame paste

1½ cups lemon juice

2 garlic cloves, finely chopped

1 tbsp chopped fresh mint

7 oz/200 g canned chickpeas, drained and rinsed

salt and pepper

chopped fresh cilantro, to garnish

extra virgin olive oil, for drizzling

warm pita bread, to serve

Jellied Vegetable Consommé

1. Heat the oil in a large pan. Add the onion and leek, stir well, cover, and cook over low heat, stirring occasionally, for 30 minutes. Add the tomatoes and mushrooms and cook for 5 minutes, then pour in the basic vegetable stock and bring to a boil. Cover and simmer for 1 hour.

2. Remove the pan from the heat, strain the stock into a bowl, pressing the vegetables with the back of a ladle to extract the liquid, stir in the yeast extract, and let cool completely. Discard the contents of the strainer.

3. Return the cooled stock to a clean pan and whisk in the egg whites. Bring to a boil over medium-low heat. When the egg white floats on the surface, reduce the heat and simmer for 1 minute. Remove from the heat and strain the stock through a cheesecloth-lined strainer into a bowl. Let cool. Pour ⅔ cup of the cooled stock into a pan, sprinkle the gelatin over the surface, and let stand for 5 minutes. (If using vegetarian gelatin, follow the package instructions.) Add 5 cups of the remaining stock and simmer over low heat, gently stirring occasionally, for 5 minutes, until the gelatin has dissolved completely. Remove the pan from the heat and let cool.

4. Stir the Madeira into the consommé and season to taste with salt and pepper. Pour into a bowl and chill in the refrigerator for 4 hours, until set. Chop the jellied consommé and spoon into individual bowls. Sprinkle with the parsley and serve immediately.

Serves 6

1 tbsp olive oil

1 small onion, finely chopped

1 leek, thinly sliced

2 tomatoes, halved crosswise

8 oz/225 g cremini mushrooms, sliced

6¾ cups basic vegetable stock

2 tsp yeast extract

2 egg whites

1 envelope (½ oz/15 g) powdered gelatin

¾ cup Madeira or medium sherry

salt and pepper

chopped fresh flat-leaf parsley, to garnish

Cucumber & Shrimp Soup

1. Pour the basic vegetable stock into a pan. Add the cucumber, scallions, and dill and bring to a boil. Reduce the heat and simmer for 20–25 minutes, until the vegetables are tender.

2. Remove the pan from the heat and let cool slightly. Ladle the soup into a food processor or blender, in batches if necessary, and process to a smooth puree.

3. Return the soup to the rinsed-out pan and reheat gently. Meanwhile, stir the cornstarch to a paste with the water in a bowl. Stir the paste into the soup and bring to a boil, stirring constantly. Reduce the heat and simmer for 3 minutes, then remove from the heat, season to taste with salt and pepper, pour into a bowl, and let cool completely.

4. Stir in a few drops of green food coloring, if using, and add the shrimp. Cover with plastic wrap and chill in the refrigerator for at least 3 hours.

5. Stir the soup and taste and adjust the seasoning, if necessary. Ladle into bowls, swirl in the cream, and serve immediately.

Serves 6

5⅔ cups basic vegetable stock

2 cucumbers, peeled, halved lengthwise, seeded, and sliced

10 scallions, chopped

1 tbsp chopped fresh dill

5 tbsp cornstarch

5 tbsp water

green food coloring (optional)

3 oz/85 g peeled cooked shrimp

6 tbsp light cream, chilled, to garnish

salt and pepper

75

Tomato & Smoked Shellfish Soup

1. Pour the basic vegetable stock into a bowl. Add the tomatoes, cucumber, shallot, vinegar, sugar, mustard, Tabasco sauce, and smoked shellfish and stir well. Season to taste with salt and pepper, cover with plastic wrap, and chill for at least 2 hours.

2. To serve, stir the soup and taste and adjust the seasoning, if necessary. Ladle into bowls, sprinkle with croutons, and serve.

Serves 6

3 cups basic vegetable stock

6 ripe tomatoes, peeled, seeded, and chopped

1 cucumber, peeled, halved lengthwise, seeded, and chopped

1 shallot, chopped

3 tbsp sherry vinegar

1 tsp sugar

1½ tsp Dijon mustard

¼ tsp Tabasco sauce or pinch of cayenne pepper

1 lb 2 oz/500 g smoked oysters or smoked mussels

salt and pepper

croutons, to serve (see page 65)

Mussel Soup

1. Scrub the mussels under cold running water and pull off the "beards." Discard any with broken shells or that do not shut immediately when sharply tapped. Put them into a large pan, pour in the basic vegetable stock and wine, and add the onion, celery, and parsley. Cover and bring to a boil over high heat. Cook, shaking the pan occasionally, for 3–5 minutes, until the shells have opened.

2. Remove the pan from the heat and lift out the mussels with a slotted spoon. Discard any that remain shut, shell the remainder, and set aside for another dish.

3. Strain the soup into a clean pan and discard the contents of the strainer. Stir in the cream and cayenne, season to taste with salt and pepper, and let cool completely. Cover with plastic wrap and chill for at least 3 hours.

4. To serve, stir the soup and taste and adjust the seasoning, if necessary. Ladle into bowls and serve immediately with garlic and herb bread.

Serves 6

36 live mussels

⅔ cup basic vegetable stock

1¼ cups dry white wine

¼ onion, finely chopped

½ celery stalk, finely chopped

5 tbsp chopped fresh flat-leaf parsley

2½ cups heavy cream

pinch of cayenne pepper or dash of Tabasco sauce

salt and pepper

garlic and herb bread, to serve

World Classics

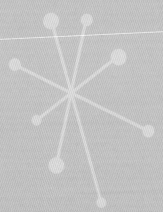

Borscht—Russia

1. Peel and coarsely grate 4 of the beets. Melt the butter in a large pan. Add the onions and cook over low heat, stirring occasionally, for 5 minutes, until softened. Add the grated beets, carrots, and celery and cook, stirring occasionally, for another 5 minutes.

2. Increase the heat to medium, add the tomatoes, vinegar, sugar, garlic, and bouquet garni, season with salt and pepper, and stir well, then pour in the basic vegetable stock and bring to a boil. Reduce the heat, cover, and simmer for 1¼ hours.

3. Meanwhile, peel and grate the remaining beet. Add it and any juices to the pan and simmer for another 10 minutes. Remove the pan from the heat and let stand for 10 minutes.

4. Remove and discard the bouquet garni. Ladle the soup into warmed bowls and top each with a spoonful of sour cream, sprinkle with chopped dill, and serve immediately with rye bread.

Serves 6

5 beets, about 2¼ lb/1 kg
5 tbsp butter
2 onions, thinly sliced
3 carrots, thinly sliced
3 celery stalks, thinly sliced
6 tomatoes, peeled, seeded, and chopped
1 tbsp red wine vinegar
1 tbsp sugar
2 garlic cloves, finely chopped
1 bouquet garni (3 fresh parsley sprigs, 2 fresh thyme sprigs, and 1 bay leaf, tied together)
5⅔ cups basic vegetable stock
salt and pepper
rye bread, to serve

To garnish
sour cream
chopped fresh dill

78

French Onion Soup

1. Heat the oil with the butter in a large pan. Add the onions, stir well, cover, and cook over very low heat, stirring occasionally, for 15 minutes. Uncover the pan, increase the heat to medium, stir in the garlic, sugar, and 1 teaspoon of salt, and cook, stirring frequently, for 30–40 minutes, until the onions are deep golden brown.

2. Meanwhile, bring the basic vegetable stock to a boil in another pan. Sprinkle the flour over the onions and cook, stirring constantly, for 3 minutes. Stir in the vermouth and cook, stirring constantly, for 2 minutes, until the alcohol has evaporated, then gradually stir in the hot stock and bring to a boil. Skim off any foam that rises to the surface, reduce the heat, cover, and simmer for 40 minutes.

3. Meanwhile, make the cheese croutes. Preheat the broiler. Toast the slices of bread on both sides. Rub each slice with the garlic clove, then top with the cheese and broil for a few minutes, until melted.

4. Stir in the brandy, remove the pan from the heat, and taste and adjust the seasoning. Ladle into warmed bowls, top each with a cheese croute, and serve immediately.

Serves 6

1 tbsp olive oil

2 tbsp butter

4–5 onions, about 1 lb 7 oz/650 g, thinly sliced

3 garlic cloves, finely chopped

1 tsp sugar

8¾ cups basic vegetable stock

2 tbsp all-purpose flour

⅔ cup dry white vermouth

3 tbsp brandy

salt and pepper

Cheese croutes

6 slices of French bread

1 garlic clove, halved

2 cups grated Gruyère cheese

Bouillabaisse—France

1. Cut the large fish into 3–4 pieces. Leave the small ones whole. Scrub the mussels under cold running water and pull of the "beards." Discard any with broken shells or that do not shut immediately when sharply tapped. Pour the basic vegetable stock into a pan and bring to a boil. Put the saffron into a bowl, pour in hot water to cover, and let soak.

2. Put the onions, leeks, celery, fennel, tomatoes, garlic, orange rind, chile, thyme sprig, bay leaves, peppercorns, and cloves into a large pan. Put the firm-fleshed fish, such as monkfish, on top, pour in half the olive oil, and season with salt. Pour in the stock, bring back to a boil, cover, and simmer for 8 minutes.

3. Add the softer fish, the remaining olive oil, and the saffron with its soaking water. Cover and simmer for another 4 minutes. Add the mussels and langoustines, cover, and cook for 4 minutes more, until the mussels have opened and all the fish is cooked. Discard any mussels that remain closed.

4. Carefully transfer the fish, shellfish, and vegetables to a warm serving dish. Strain the broth into a warmed tureen and taste and adjust the seasoning, if necessary. Serve the fish and broth immediately.

Serves 8

5 lb/2.25 kg mixed fish, such as monkfish, red snapper, and whiting

1 lb/450 g mussels

15 cups basic vegetable stock

½ tsp saffron threads

2 onions, chopped

2 leeks, white parts only, chopped

3 celery stalks, chopped

1 fennel bulb, sliced

2 large tomatoes, peeled and chopped

4 garlic cloves, finely chopped

1 strip of thinly pared orange rind

1 red chile, seeded and chopped

1 fresh thyme sprig

2 bay leaves

8 black peppercorns

2 cloves

1 cup olive oil

1 lb/450 g cooked langoustines

salt and pepper

Bauernsuppe—Germany

1. Melt the butter in a large pan. Add the meat and cook over medium heat, stirring frequently, for 8–10 minutes, until lightly browned all over. Meanwhile, bring the basic vegetable stock to a boil in another pan.

2. Add the onions to the meat, reduce the heat, and cook, stirring frequently, for 5 minutes, until softened. Add the garlic and cook for another 2 minutes. Stir in the paprika and flour and cook, stirring constantly, for 3–4 minutes. Gradually stir in the hot basic vegetable stock and bring to a boil. Add the bouquet garni, season with salt, cover, and simmer, stirring occasionally, for 1 hour.

3. Add the potatoes to the soup, re-cover the pan, and simmer for another 45 minutes, until the meat and vegetables are tender.

4. Remove the pan from the heat and taste and adjust the seasoning, if necessary. Remove and discard the bouquet garni. Ladle the soup into warmed bowls, sprinkle with the dill and grated cheese, and serve immediately.

Serves 6

4 tbsp butter

2¼ lb/1 kg stewing steak, trimmed of fat and cut into ¾-inch/2-cm cubes

11¼ cups basic vegetable stock

2 onions, chopped

1 garlic clove, finely chopped

1 tsp paprika

4 tbsp all-purpose flour

1 bouquet garni (3 fresh parsley sprigs, 2 fresh thyme sprigs, and 1 bay leaf, tied together)

3 potatoes, diced

salt

To garnish

2 tsp chopped fresh dill

½ cup grated Gruyère cheese

81

Minestrone—Italy

1. Heat the oil in a large pan. Add the onion, garlic, celery, and bacon, and cook over low heat, stirring occasionally, for 5–7 minutes, until the onion has softened and the bacon is crisp. Stir in the cabbage and cook, stirring frequently, for another 5 minutes.

2. Increase the heat to medium, pour in the wine, and cook for about 2 minutes, until the alcohol has evaporated, then pour in the basic vegetable stock. Add the cannellini beans and bring to a boil, then lower the heat, cover, and simmer for 2½ hours.

3. Add the tomatoes, tomato paste, sugar, carrots, peas, green beans, pasta, and herbs and season to taste with salt and pepper. Simmer for 20–25 minutes, until the pasta is cooked and the vegetables are tender.

4. Ladle the soup into warmed bowls and serve immediately, passing around the grated cheese separately.

Serves 6

2 tbsp olive oil

1 Bermuda onion, chopped

2 garlic cloves, finely chopped

2 celery stalks, chopped

4 slices of bacon, diced

½ small white cabbage, cored and shredded

⅔ cup red wine

7½ cups basic vegetable stock

⅓ cup dried cannellini beans, soaked overnight in cold water to cover, and drained

4 plum tomatoes, peeled, seeded, and chopped

2 tbsp tomato paste

2 tsp sugar

2 carrots, diced

½ cup fresh shelled peas

2 oz/55 g green beans, cut into short lengths

½ cup ziti pasta

2 tbsp chopped fresh mixed herbs

salt and pepper

grated Parmesan cheese, to serve

Fabada—Spain

1. Bring the basic vegetable stock to a boil in a large pan. Add the beans, onion, and garlic and bring back to a boil, then reduce the heat, cover, and simmer for 1 hour, until the beans are tender.

2. Meanwhile, put the saffron into a small bowl, add water to cover, and let soak.

3. Add the sausages, bacon, ham, thyme, and saffron with its soaking water to the pan, season to taste with salt and pepper, and mix well. Re-cover and simmer the soup for another 30–35 minutes. Ladle into warmed bowls and serve immediately.

Serves 6

7½ cups basic vegetable stock

1¼ cups dried lima beans, soaked overnight in cold water to cover, and drained

1¼ cups dried large white kidney beans (fabes de la granja) or cannellini beans, soaked overnight in water to cover, and drained

1 Bermuda onion, chopped

2 garlic cloves, finely chopped

pinch of saffron threads

4 oz/125 g morcilla or other blood sausage, sliced

2 chorizo sausages, sliced

4 slices of bacon, diced

⅓ cup diced smoked ham

pinch of dried thyme

salt and pepper

Caldo Verde—Portugal

1. Heat 2 tablespoons of the olive oil in a large pan. Add the onion and garlic and cook over low heat, stirring occasionally, for 5 minutes, until softened. Add the potatoes and cook, stirring constantly, for 3 minutes more.

2. Increase the heat to medium, pour in the basic vegetable stock, and bring to a boil. Reduce the heat, cover, and cook for 10 minutes.

3. Meanwhile, heat the remaining olive oil in a skillet. Add the sausage slices and cook over low heat, turning occasionally, for a few minutes, until the fat runs. Remove with a slotted spoon and drain on paper towels.

4. Remove the pan of soup from the heat and mash the potatoes with a potato masher. Return to the heat, add the kale, and bring back to a boil. Reduce the heat and simmer for 5–6 minutes, until tender.

5. Remove the pan from the heat and mash the potatoes again to incorporate. Stir in the sausage slices, season to taste with salt and pepper, and ladle into warmed bowls. Drizzle each with a little olive oil and serve immediately.

Serves 6

3 tbsp olive oil, plus extra for drizzling

1 Bermuda onion, finely chopped

2 garlic cloves, finely chopped

3¼ cups diced potatoes

6¾ cups basic vegetable stock

4½ oz/125 g chorizo or other spicy sausage, thinly sliced

5 cups finely shredded kale or savoy cabbage

salt and pepper

84

London Particular—England

1. Dice 6 slices of the bacon. Melt the butter in a pan. Add the diced bacon and cook over low heat, stirring frequently, for 4–5 minutes. Add the onions, carrots, and celery and cook, stirring frequently, for another 5 minutes.

2. Increase the heat to medium, add the peas, pour in the basic vegetable stock, and bring to a boil. Reduce the heat, cover, and simmer for 1 hour.

3. Meanwhile, preheat the broiler. Broil the remaining bacon for 2–4 minutes on each side, until crisp, then remove from the heat. Let cool slightly, then crumble.

4. Remove the soup from the heat and season to taste with salt and pepper. Ladle into warmed bowls, garnish with the crumbled bacon and the croutons, and serve immediately.

Serves 6

8 thick slices of bacon

2 tbsp butter

2 onions, chopped

2 carrots, chopped

2 celery stalks, chopped

generous ½ cup yellow split peas, soaked in cold water for 1–2 hours, and drained

7½ cups basic vegetable stock

salt and pepper

croutons, to garnish (see page 65)

Cullen Skink—Scotland

1. Put the fish, onion, and parsley into a large pan, pour in the basic vegetable stock, and bring to a boil, skimming off the foam that rises to the surface. Reduce the heat, cover, and simmer for 10 minutes, until the flesh flakes easily.

2. Remove the pan from the heat and lift out the fish with a slotted spatula. Remove and discard the skin and bones and flake the flesh. Strain the basic vegetable stock into a clean pan.

3. Return the pan to the heat, add the potatoes, and bring back to a boil. Reduce the heat and simmer for 20–30 minutes, until tender.

4. Remove the pan from the heat. Using a slotted spoon, transfer the potatoes to a bowl, add the butter, and mash until smooth.

5. Return the pan to the heat, add the milk, and bring to a boil. Whisk in the mashed potatoes, a little at a time, until thoroughly incorporated. Gently stir in the fish and season to taste with salt and pepper. Ladle into warmed bowls, sprinkle with chopped parsley, and serve immediately with crusty bread.

Serves 6

1 lb 2 oz/500 g smoked white fish (traditionally smoked haddock)

1 large onion, chopped

4 fresh parsley sprigs

5⅔ cups basic vegetable stock

1 lb 10 oz/750 g potatoes, cut into chunks

4 tbsp butter

3¾ cups milk

salt and pepper

chopped fresh flat-leaf parsley, to garnish

crusty bread, to serve

Mussel Soup—Ireland

1. Scrub the mussels under cold running water and pull of the "beards." Discard any with broken shells or that do not shut when sharply tapped. Sprinkle the onion, parsley, and bay leaves over the bottom of a large pan, put the mussels on top, season with pepper, and pour in the hard cider. Cover, bring to a boil over high heat, and cook, shaking the pan occasionally, for 4–5 minutes, until the mussels have opened. Remove the pan from the heat and lift out the mussels. Discard any that remain shut. Remove the mussels from the shells and set aside. Strain the cooking liquid into a bowl.

2. Melt the butter in a large pan. Add the celery and leeks and cook over low heat, stirring occasionally, for 8 minutes, until lightly browned. Meanwhile, pour the milk into another pan and bring just to a boil, then remove from the heat.

3. Sprinkle the flour over the vegetables and cook, stirring constantly, for 2 minutes. Increase the heat to medium and gradually stir in the milk, a little at a time, then stir in the basic vegetable stock. Bring to a boil, stirring constantly, then reduce the heat, and simmer for 15 minutes.

4. Remove the pan from the heat and strain the soup into a bowl. Return to the rinsed-out pan, add the reserved cooking liquid, the nutmeg, fennel seeds, and mussels, and season to taste with salt and pepper. Return to the heat and stir in the cream. Reheat gently for a few minutes but do not let the soup boil. Ladle into warmed bowls and serve with whole wheat bread.

Serves 6

48 mussels

1 onion, finely chopped

2 tbsp chopped fresh flat-leaf parsley

2 bay leaves

generous 1 cup hard cider

4 tbsp butter

2 celery stalks, chopped

2 leeks, thinly sliced

2½ cups milk

⅓ cup all-purpose flour

2½ cups basic vegetable stock

pinch of grated nutmeg

½ tsp fennel seeds

1 cup heavy cream

salt and pepper

whole wheat bread, to serve

87

Avgolemono—Greece

1. Pour the basic vegetable stock into a large pan and bring to a boil. Add the rice, bring back to a boil, then reduce the heat, and simmer for 15 minutes, until the rice is tender.

2. Meanwhile, beat the eggs in a bowl and gradually beat in the lemon juice. Gradually beat in a ladleful of the hot soup, then add the mixture to the pan. Cook over low heat, rotating the pan occasionally to distribute the egg and lemon sauce evenly, for 2–3 minutes.

3. Remove from the heat, season the soup to taste with pepper, and ladle into warmed bowls. Sprinkle with parsley and serve immediately.

Serves 6

* 7½ cups basic vegetable stock
generous ½ cup long-grain rice
4 eggs
½ cup lemon juice
pepper
chopped fresh flat-leaf parsley, to garnish

Harira—North Africa

1. Heat the olive oil in a large pan. Add the lamb and cook over medium heat, stirring frequently, for 8–10 minutes, until lightly browned all over. Reduce the heat, add the onion, and cook, stirring frequently, for 5 minutes, until softened.

2. Increase the heat to medium, add the chickpeas, pour in the basic vegetable stock, and bring to a boil. Reduce the heat, cover, and simmer for 2 hours.

3. Stir in the lentils, tomatoes, bell pepper, tomato paste, sugar, cinnamon, turmeric, ginger, cilantro, and parsley and simmer for another 15 minutes. Add the rice and simmer for an additional 15 minutes, until the rice is cooked and the lentils are tender.

4. Season to taste with salt and pepper and remove the pan from the heat. Ladle the soup into warmed bowls, sprinkle with a little chopped cilantro, and serve immediately.

Serves 6

2 tbsp olive oil

8 oz/225 g boneless lean lamb, cut into cubes

1 onion, chopped

½ cup dried chickpeas, soaked overnight in water to cover, and drained

6¾ cups basic vegetable stock

½ cup red or yellow lentils

2 large tomatoes, peeled, seeded, and diced

1 red bell pepper, seeded and diced

1 tbsp tomato paste

1 tsp sugar

1 tsp ground cinnamon

½ tsp ground turmeric

½ tsp ground ginger

1 tbsp chopped fresh cilantro, plus extra to garnish

1 tbsp chopped fresh flat-leaf parsley

scant ⅓ cup long-grain rice

salt and pepper

Eshkaneh—Iran

1. Melt the butter in a large pan. Add the onions and cook over low heat, stirring occasionally, for 7–8 minutes, until just beginning to color.

2. Sprinkle in the flour and cook, stirring constantly, for 2 minutes. Remove the pan from the heat and gradually stir in the basic vegetable stock, a little at a time. Return the pan to medium heat and bring to a boil, stirring constantly. Add the turmeric, lemon juice, sugar, and cilantro and season generously with salt and pepper. Reduce the heat, cover, and simmer for 10 minutes.

3. Lightly beat the egg in a bowl. Whisk it into the soup and remove the pan from the heat. Ladle into warmed bowls and serve immediately with warm flat bread.

Serves 6

4 tbsp butter
4 onions, thinly sliced
2 tbsp all-purpose flour
✳ 5 cups basic vegetable stock
1 tsp ground turmeric
½ cup lemon juice
1 tbsp superfine sugar
1 tbsp chopped fresh cilantro
1 egg
salt and pepper
warm flat bread, to serve

90

Wonton Soup—China

1. Combine the pork, shrimp, scallion, ginger, sugar, rice wine, and half the soy sauce in a bowl until thoroughly mixed. Cover and let marinate for 20 minutes.

2. Put 1 tsp of the mixture in the center of each wonton wrapper. Dampen the edges, fold corner to corner into a triangle, and press to seal, then seal the bottom corners together.

3. Bring the basic vegetable stock to a boil in a large pan. Add the wontons and cook for 5 minutes. Stir in the remaining soy sauce and remove from the heat. Ladle the soup and wontons into warmed bowls, sprinkle with snipped chives, and serve immediately.

Serves 6

6 oz/175 g pork or chicken, ground

2 oz/55 g peeled shrimp, ground

1 finely chopped scallion

1 tsp finely chopped fresh ginger

1 tsp sugar

1 tbsp Chinese rice wine or dry sherry

2 tbsp light soy sauce

24 store-bought wonton wrappers

3¾ cups basic vegetable stock

snipped fresh chives, to garnish

Three Delicacy Soup—China

1. Combine the chicken and shrimp in a bowl. Mix the cornstarch to a paste with the water in another bowl and add to the mixture, together with the egg white and a pinch of salt, stirring well to coat.

2. Bring the basic vegetable stock to a boil in a pan over medium heat. Add the chicken mixture and the ham and bring back to a boil. Reduce the heat and simmer for 1 minute. Taste and adjust the seasoning, if necessary, and remove from the heat. Ladle into warmed bowls, garnish with scallions, and serve immediately.

Serves 6

6 oz/175 g skinless boneless chicken breast portion, very thinly sliced into strips

6 oz/175 g peeled shrimp, halved if large

1 tsp cornstarch

2 tsp water

1 medium egg white, lightly beaten

✳ 4 cups basic vegetable stock

6 oz/175 g honey-roast ham, very thinly sliced into strips

salt

chopped scallions or snipped fresh chives, to garnish

Seaweed Soup with Miso—Japan

1. Heat the oil in a pan. Add the onion and garlic and cook over low heat, stirring occasionally, for 5 minutes, until softened. Meanwhile, pour the basic vegetable stock into another pan and bring to a boil.

2. Stir the miso paste, tomato paste, ginger, and coriander into the onion mixture, mixing well, then add the carrots, and cook, stirring frequently, for 5 minutes. If the mixture looks as if it might scorch, stir in 1–2 tablespoons of the hot stock.

3. Add the yaki-nori to the stock, then stir in the onion mixture, and simmer gently for 10 minutes. Ladle into warmed bowls and serve immediately, garnished with snipped chives.

Serves 6

1 tbsp sunflower oil
1 large onion, thinly sliced
2 garlic cloves, finely chopped
7½ cups basic vegetable stock
1½ tbsp red miso paste
1 tbsp tomato paste
1 tsp ground ginger
1 tsp ground coriander
2 carrots, thinly sliced
3 sheets yaki-nori seaweed
(seasoned and toasted nori
seaweed), torn into shreds
snipped fresh chives,
to garnish

93

Crab Soup—Vietnam

1. Put the mushrooms into a bowl, pour in the water, and let soak for 20 minutes. Meanwhile, chop the white parts of the scallions and thinly slice the green parts diagonally. Slice the asparagus diagonally into ¾-inch/2-cm pieces. Pick over the crabmeat and remove any pieces of shell and cartilage.

2. Drain the mushrooms, reserving the soaking liquid, and squeeze gently to remove the excess liquid. Remove and discard the stalks and thinly slice the caps. Strain the soaking liquid through a cheesecloth-lined strainer.

3. Heat the oil in a large pan. Add the chopped scallions and garlic and stir-fry over medium heat for 2 minutes. Pour in the basic vegetable stock and reserved soaking liquid, add the mushrooms, and bring to a boil.

4. Stir in 1 tablespoon of the Thai fish sauce, add the sliced scallions and asparagus pieces, and bring back to a boil. Reduce the heat and simmer for 5 minutes, then gently stir in the crabmeat and cilantro. Simmer for another 3–4 minutes to heat through.

5. Remove the pan from the heat, taste, and stir in more fish sauce, if necessary. Ladle into warmed bowls and serve immediately.

Serves 6

6 dried shiitake mushrooms

1½ cups hot water

5 scallions

12 oz/350 g asparagus spears, trimmed

1 lb 10 oz/750 g white crabmeat, thawed if frozen

2 tbsp peanut oil

3 garlic cloves, finely chopped

7½ cups basic vegetable stock

1–2 tbsp Thai fish sauce

3 tbsp chopped fresh cilantro

Laksa—Malaysia

1. Peel the shrimp, reserving the heads and shells. Devein the shrimp by cutting a slit along their backs with a sharp knife and removing the black thread with the point of the knife. Rinse the heads and shells. Heat 1 tablespoon of the oil in a pan. Add the shrimp heads and shells and stir-fry over medium heat for 2–3 minutes, until lightly colored, then pour in the basic vegetable stock and bring to a boil. Reduce the heat and simmer for 15 minutes. Strain the stock into a bowl and discard the shrimp shells.

2. Combine the curry paste and ground nuts in a bowl. Heat the remaining oil in a pan. Add the curry paste and cook over low heat, stirring frequently, for 4–5 minutes. Increase the heat to medium, pour in the basic vegetable stock, and bring to a boil, then reduce the heat, cover, and simmer for 20 minutes.

3. Meanwhile, put the noodles into a bowl, pour in boiling water to cover, and let soak for 5 minutes, then drain. Blanch the bean sprouts in boiling salted water for a few minutes, then drain. Whisk the coconut milk into the pan and simmer for 2 minutes, then add the shrimp, squid, and sugar, and season to taste with salt. Simmer for 5 minutes, until the shrimp and squid are tender, then remove from the heat. Divide the noodles and bean sprouts among warmed bowls and ladle the soup over them. Garnish with chopped cilantro, cucumber strips, and scallions, and serve immediately.

Serves 6

12 oz/350 g large shrimp

6 tbsp peanut oil

5⅔ cups basic vegetable stock

2 tbsp Panang curry paste (very hot) or red curry paste (hot)

¼ cup candlenuts or cashew nuts, ground

9 oz/250 g rice noodles

3 cups bean sprouts

2½ cups canned coconut milk

6 oz/175 g prepared squid, scored and cut into small diamonds

1 tbsp brown sugar

salt

To garnish
fresh cilantro sprigs

julienne strips of cucumber

chopped scallions

Tom Yam Goong—Thailand

1. Peel the shrimp, reserving the heads and shells. Devein the shrimp by cutting a slit along their backs with a sharp knife and removing the black thread with the point of the knife. Rinse the heads and shells.

2. Pour the basic vegetable stock into a pan, add the shrimp heads and tails, lemongrass, kaffir lime leaves, and a pinch of salt, and bring to a boil. Reduce the heat and simmer for 10 minutes. Remove the pan from the heat and strain into a clean pan.

3. Return the pan to the heat, add the green chiles, and bring back to a boil, then reduce the heat and simmer for another 10 minutes. Stir in the Thai fish sauce and shrimp and simmer for 5 minutes. Add the scallions, lime juice, and red chiles, and heat through for 1–2 minutes.

4. Remove the pan from the heat and taste and adjust the seasoning with more lime juice, fish sauce, or salt, if necessary. Ladle into warmed bowls, sprinkle with the cilantro, and serve immediately with the lime wedges.

Serves 6

1 lb 2 oz/500 g large shrimp

6¾ cups stock

3 lemongrass stalks bruised

6 kaffir lime leaves, torn

3 green chiles, seeded and thinly sliced

3 tbsp Thai fish sauce

3 scallions, chopped

2 tbsp lime juice

2 red chiles, seeded and thinly sliced

1 tbsp chopped fresh cilantro

salt

lime wedges, to serve

96

Chicken Soup with Ginger & Coconut Milk—Thailand

1. Put the chicken, rice, lemongrass, garlic, chiles, lime leaves, ginger, and cilantro into a pan, pour in the basic vegetable stock and coconut milk, and bring to a boil over medium heat, stirring occasionally. Reduce the heat, cover, and simmer for 1 hour.

2. Remove the pan from the heat and let cool slightly. Remove and discard the lemongrass and kaffir lime leaves. Ladle the soup into a food processor or blender, in batches if necessary, and process to a puree.

3. Return the soup to the rinsed-out pan, season to taste with salt, and add the scallions, corn cobs, and mushrooms. Bring back to a boil, then reduce the heat, and simmer for 5 minutes.

4. Remove the pan from the heat. Ladle the soup into warmed bowls, garnish with chopped cilantro and chile, and serve immediately.

Serves 6

14 oz/400g skinless, boneless chicken breast portions, cut into strips

½ cup Thai fragrant rice

1 lemongrass stalk, bruised

4 garlic cloves, coarsely chopped

2 green chiles, seeded and sliced

4 kaffir lime leaves, torn

1-inch/2.5-cm piece fresh ginger, chopped

4 tbsp chopped fresh cilantro, plus extra to garnish

6¾ cups basic vegetable stock

1¾ cups canned coconut milk

4 scallions, thinly sliced

1 cup baby corn cobs

4 oz/115 g white mushrooms, halved

salt

chopped red chile, to garnish

Manhattan Clam Chowder—United States

1. Heat the oil in a pan. Add the salt pork and cook over medium heat, stirring frequently, for 6–8 minutes, until golden brown. Remove with a slotted spoon.

2. Add the onion and celery to the pan, reduce the heat to low, and cook, stirring occasionally, for 5 minutes, until softened. Increase the heat to medium, add the tomatoes, potatoes, thyme, and parsley, return the pork to the pan, season with salt and pepper, and pour in the tomato juice and basic vegetable stock. Bring to a boil, stirring constantly, then reduce the heat, cover, and simmer for 15–20 minutes, until the potatoes are just tender.

3. Meanwhile, scrub the clams under cold running water. Discard any with broken shells or that do not shut when sharply tapped. Put them into a pan, pour in the wine, cover, and cook over high heat, shaking the pan occasionally, for 4–5 minutes, until the shells have opened.

4. Remove the clams with a slotted spoon and let cool slightly. Discard any clams that remain shut. Strain the cooking liquid through a cheesecloth-lined strainer into the soup. Remove the clams from the shells.

5. Add the clams to the soup and heat through, stirring constantly, for 2–3 minutes. Remove from the heat and taste and adjust the seasoning, if necessary. Ladle into warmed bowls and serve immediately with crusty bread.

Serves 6

1 tsp sunflower oil
4 oz/115 g salt pork or unsmoked bacon, diced
1 onion, finely chopped
2 celery stalks, chopped
4 tomatoes, peeled, seeded, and chopped
3 potatoes, diced
pinch of dried thyme
3 tbsp chopped fresh parsley
⅔ cup tomato juice
2½ cups basic vegetable stock
36 quahog or littleneck clams
⅔ cups dry white wine
salt and pepper
crusty bread, to serve

Chicken & Corn Soup—United States

1. Remove the skin from the chicken, cut the meat off the bones, and cut into small pieces. Put the saffron into a bowl, pour in hot water to cover, and let soak.

2. Heat the oil in a pan. Add the onions and celery and cook over low heat, stirring occasionally, for 5 minutes, until softened. Increase the heat to medium, pour in the basic vegetable stock, add the peppercorns and mace, and bring to a boil. Reduce the heat and simmer for 25 minutes.

3. Increase the heat to medium, add the chicken, noodles, corn, sage, parsley, and saffron with its soaking water, season to taste with salt and pepper, and bring back to a boil. Reduce the heat and simmer for another 20 minutes.

4. Remove the pan from the heat, taste and adjust the seasoning, if necessary, ladle into warmed bowls, and serve immediately.

Serves 6

1 roasted chicken, about
   3 lb/1.3 kg
½ tsp saffron threads
3 tbsp corn oil
2 onions, thinly sliced
3 celery stalks, sliced
7½ cups basic vegetable stock
8 black peppercorns
1 mace blade
4 oz/115 g egg noodles
2⅓ cups frozen corn
pinch of dried sage
2 tbsp chopped fresh flat-leaf
   parsley
salt and pepper

99

Jamaican Pepper Pot—Caribbean

1. Put the steak, pork, and callaloo into a large pan, pour in the basic vegetable stock, and bring to a boil over medium heat. Reduce the heat and simmer for 2–2¼ hours, until the meat is tender. Meanwhile, cut off the stems of fresh okra, if using, being careful not to pierce the pods. Dip the cut ends into salt and let drain in a colander for 30 minutes. Rinse well in water mixed with the lemon juice. If using frozen okra, rinse in water mixed with the lemon juice.

2. Make the plantain chips. Using a sharp knife, cut through the plantain skins along the ridges and peel off. Cut the flesh into wafer-thin slices with a mandoline or very sharp knife, put into a bowl of ice water, and let soak for 30 minutes. Heat the oil in a deep-fryer to 360–375°F/180–190°C, or until a cube of day-old bread browns in 30 seconds. Drain the plantain slices and pat dry with a dish towel. Dust with the cinnamon, add to the hot oil, in batches if necessary, and cook until golden brown. Remove with a slotted spoon and drain on paper towels.

3. Add the okra, sweet potato, christophine, chile, coconut milk, and scallions to the pan with the stock, season with salt and pepper, and bring back to a boil. Simmer for 35–40 minutes, until all the vegetables are tender and the soup has thickened. Remove the pan from the heat and taste and adjust the seasoning, if necessary. Ladle into warmed bowls and serve immediately, passing around the plantain chips separately.

Serves 6

8 oz/225 g stewing steak, diced

8 oz/225 g salt pork, diced

8 oz/225 g callaloo or spinach, coarse stalks removed, finely chopped

12½ cups basic vegetable stock

8 oz/225 g fresh or frozen okra

1 tbsp lemon juice

8 oz/225 g sweet potato, sliced

8 oz/225 g christophine (chayote), peeled and thinly sliced

1 green chile, seeded and sliced

3 cups canned coconut milk

2 scallions, finely chopped

salt and pepper

Plantain chips
2 plantains

ice water

ground cinnamon, for dusting

vegetable oil, for deep-frying

100

Black Bean Soup—Caribbean

1. Heat the oil in a large pan. Add the onion, celery, and garlic and cook over low heat, stirring occasionally, for 6–8 minutes, until softened.

2. Increase the heat to medium, add the beans, pour in the basic vegetable stock, and bring to a boil. Reduce the heat, cover, and simmer for 2–2½ hours, until the beans are tender.

3. Remove the pan from the heat and let cool slightly. Ladle all or half the soup, depending on the texture you require, into a food processor or blender, in batches if necessary, and process to a puree.

4. Return the soup to the pan and bring just to a boil. If it is very thick, add a little more stock or water. Stir in the cayenne, lemon juice, vinegar, sherry, and hard-cooked eggs and season to taste with salt and pepper. Reduce the heat and simmer, stirring constantly, for 10 minutes.

5. Remove the pan from the heat and ladle the soup into warmed bowls. Garnish with celery leaves and serve immediately, passing around the grated cheese separately.

Serves 6

3 tbsp corn oil

1 large onion, chopped

2 celery stalks, chopped

2 garlic cloves, chopped

2½ cups dried black beans or black-eyed peas, soaked overnight in cold water to cover, and drained

11¼ cups basic vegetable stock

¾ tsp cayenne pepper

5 tbsp lemon juice

2 tbsp red wine vinegar

2 tbsp dry sherry

4 hard-cooked eggs, coarsely chopped

salt and pepper

chopped celery leaves, to garnish

grated cheddar cheese, to serve